A Golfer's Beatitude

John Fincher

Front Cover Art by Jeri Campbell

Publisher's Notes

This is a work of fiction. Names, characters, businesses, places, events and incidents are either the products of the author's imagination or used in a fictitious manner. Any resemblance to actual persons, living or dead, or actual events is purely coincidental.

ISBN 978-1-943658-08-4
TREATY OAK PUBLISHERS

Manufactured in The United States of America.

This book is dedicated to
the Hondurans
of the Agalta Valley
and the late
Pastor Ron Campbell
who showed many persons
how to act justly,
love mercy
and walk humbly
with God.

Contents

1.

Blessed are the poor in spirit, for theirs is the Kingdom of Heaven.

Juan Jose's rivers of sweat poured forth, bubbling from beneath his skin like a hot spring through the sun worn cracks on his forehead, as he mightily swung his sickle to and fro, steady as the beat of a metronome. The scorching Honduran sun and thick oppressive humidity encapsulated his body like the fiery foil wrapped tightly around a hot baked potato lying deep within red-burning embers. He prayed fervently as he rhythmically swung back and forth to and fro. Although the arduous task of leveling the tall stalks of grain stretched many miles before him, he felt no remorse for the tedious labor performed daily in his job. Instead, he was grateful for the opportunity to work, even if it was for just a few *lempiras* per day.

Juan Jose prayed out loud, "*Dios*, I am a sinner and have done nothing to deserve Your great mercy. Thank You for the gift of my niece Angelina. I seek Your guidance for me. I am Yours and I commit my will to You. Lead me in the paths of Thy righteousness. I can do nothing by myself, but everything through You Who strengthens me. I will try to be humble in all that I do and allow Your Holy Spirit to guide me. Thank You for bringing Jaime to this valley to teach us about Your Holy Son Jesus."

Juan Jose prayed unceasingly as his sickle blade swung like the pendulum of a giant grandfather clock tilted sideways, as the seconds slowly ticked by into hours, the scintillating sun moving slowly across the azure sky. His hardened muscles responded again and again to the rhythm of his swinging as he labored on, moving quicker down the rows than any of the other workers. For ten years he had been using this tool, swinging back and forth, back and forth to an inner cadence deep within his soul. He had learned how to block the negative thoughts of the burning heat, boredom and fatigue from his mind and to find joy in only the swinging. Just recently, since Jaime had brought the gospel to his village and helped establish the church, Juan Jose added prayer to his rhythm.

He continued, "…and *Dios*, I pray for all the children of our valley, that they would have enough to eat this day. I pray that those who are sick would be healed."

The sickle and Juan Jose became linked as one tool moving up and down the rolling fields. Using the muscles of his legs, shoulders and hips he turned back and forth, back and forth, with his arms merely following the commands of these larger muscles, always swinging the same in perfect rhythm.

Tim Bigelow, the large Anglo American overseer pointed his index finger toward the field and spoke to the small Honduran landowner who looked the size of a small child alongside him. Tim had a gaping space between the thick pointing finger and his ring finger since his middle finger was only a one-inch-nub cut cleanly just below where the knuckle had been. He had come to Honduras to seek adventure while escaping his darkened past. Tim stood six foot five, weighed two hundred and seventy-seven pounds and towered menacingly over all of the shorter Hondurans. His stringy long gray hair, straggly beard that looked like dirty moss hanging from a giant tree, large beer gut that hung well beneath his waist like an over-inflated balloon, and ever present frown made him an intimidating angry giant ready to strike and crush like a thick python snake, snuffing the life out of lesser beings, devouring and slithering away.

"He's a working machine. A happy idiot, swinging his worthless life away," Tim uttered downward to the handsome landowner, Carlos Alamonzo.

Tim's words "worthless life" triggered another painful memory haunting his consciousness as he thought back to the small Crystal Beach, Texas shanty house that his single parent Samantha had raised him in. He remembered picking up the empty vodka bottles and how he had placed a shabby blanket over his mother who lay crumpled up like a dirty towel on the bathroom floor near the toilet. Even now, Tim could still remember the peculiar smell of the soiled musty house and how hiding under the threadbare covers on his bed would make the scene disappear from his eyes but the filthy house odor would not vacate his nose.

"The world needs more of the poor to be like Juan Jose. Think how much more wealthy you could become from their toil," said Tim to Carlos.

Carlos was one of the few "haves" in a country populated mostly with "have nots." His father Sergio had connections long ago. He had been rewarded for his loyalty to the people in power who sold him thousands of acres of land costing him almost nothing.

Tim Bigelow stated, "Yep, if I had ten Juan Jose's we could tame every jungle in Olancho. We could make Honduras one big coffee bean farm, and grow a little special tobacky too."

Tim remembered making drug deals in darkened bars on Galveston Island. Marijuana, cocaine, barbiturates and crystal methamphetamine became a part of his daily routine until he squandered a large advance of mobster's money on a Houston pro football game. He glanced down at his missing middle finger that he had made the mistake of lifting in defiance to the gun and knife wielding gangster bill collector. Tim could still feel the thug's blade slicing through and see his attacker bent over with his gun pointed toward Tim's head, picking up his severed finger and tossing it into the wharf water for the hungry crabs below.

"You will never find another Juan Jose. He's one of a kind," said Carlos.

"Watch this. I'm gonna mess with his mind," said Tim. "Hey, Juan Jose, come here!"

Juan Jose's prayer was broken by the loud voice and he looked across the field toward Tim. He began to walk swiftly toward Tim and Carlos.

"Yes?" said Juan Jose as he approached the two.

"You been staying up too late, Juan? Or are you drinking on the job? Your work looks sloppy and you're slow on getting it done!"

Juan Jose looked truly hurt by the comments about his work as he said, "My apologies if my work displeases you. I go to bed early and I do not drink, and I am trying my very best to do as much work as possible and to do a good job."

"You're lazy and stupid. You work slow and think even slower. If you can't go any faster, then I'm going to fire you. Now, get back to work, you thief who is stealing our time and money!"

Juan Jose turned away sadly. As he walked back to the field he began praying, "Oh God, give me the strength to do more. I must keep my job to help buy food for my widowed sister and Angelina. I am Your servant, God. Show me what You want me to do. Even I, a poor peasant from a poor village, completely undeserving of Your great mercy, can help You build Your Kingdom. Lead me. Guide me onto

Your path in the way that leads to life and please allow me to be the answer to someone's prayer."

Carlos turned to Tim and said, "I think you hurt his pride. If he ever quits, I will hold you personally responsible."

"He's not quitting. He needs the money to survive. Watch him now."

As Carlos turned back toward the field, Juan Jose began to swing his sickle powerfully. *Swoosh, swoosh* the blade knifed through the air and the grain fell to the earth almost as rapidly as a combine machine leveling stalks on a modern farm.

"He's incredible," said Carlos.

"Don't ever tell him that. I like to make him think he's worthless."

"Just keep him swinging like a mad man, and make sure he doesn't quit or die in the field," laughed Carlos.

"I have a great idea. Let's see how he can wield a chain saw tomorrow. With that amount of energy he can cut down the whole forest," said Tim.

Juan Jose swung the sickle passionately but with a steady rhythm like a high performance race car out front on the track to win. The other laborers in the field were swinging their tools at half the cadence of Juan Jose's. Sweat pooled off his head, neck, arms and legs as he sweltered to increasing degrees in the hot, humid Honduran air. Even when he reached for his makeshift water bottle that once had been a plastic oil container, he kept swinging with one arm as he drank with the other.

"Most gracious Heavenly Father, forgive me for the unkind thoughts I had concerning Señor Carlos and Señor Tim. Let me be grateful for the job I have that puts coins in my pocket to help provide for myself, my sister and my niece. I am not worthy of Your salvation and grace that have come to me," prayed Juan Jose.

Swish, swish, swish, sounded his sickle as he continued

to level the field until the sun began to set behind the mountains with the sky reflecting its waning brilliant orange glow.

Tim Bigelow took the old policeman's whistle tied with twine that hung down to his bulging chest from around his thick leather-like neck and blew three sharp shrills and the workers stopped for the day, immediately coming to rest with their sickles. They formed a line and waited for the coins that might give them enough to buy a morsel of meat to go into their soup or rice and beans that evening, if they chose to use the money wisely on food instead of vices. Juan Jose stopped intentionally and let those men who lived the farthest go before him so they might get a head start on their long trek home to their villages and loved ones.

The distant mountains began their purple glow as the setting sun made the clouds around them blossom into a pink-orange splendor. Juan Jose never failed to appreciate the beauty of his favorite time of day as he strode purposefully toward his village. He stopped by the village butcher and gave her a few Honduran *lempira* coins in exchange for a piece of pork to add to his sister María's soup for the evening.

As he ducked into her small adobe hut, Juan Jose was looking at the walls in admiration instead of at his feet where the chickens scattered, darting around on the dirt floor to escape being stepped on. María had decorated her wall with handwritten pieces of paper that contained her favorite scriptures. The papers stuck to the walls read:

Psalm 121:1-2 - I lift my eyes up to the hills. Where does my help come from? My help comes from Yahweh, who made heaven and earth.

Philippians 4:13 - I can do all things through Christ, who strengthens me.

2 Timothy 4:7 - I have fought the good fight. I have finished the course. I have kept the faith.

Romans 1:16-17 - For I am not ashamed of the Good News of Christ, because it is the power of God for salvation for everyone who believes, for the Jew first and also for the Greek. For in it is revealed God's righteousness from faith to faith. As it is written, "But the righteous shall live by faith."

John 12:46 - I have come as a light into the world, that whoever believes in me may not remain in the darkness.

Joshua 1:9 - Haven't I commanded you? Be strong and courageous. Don't be afraid. Don't be dismayed, for Yahweh your God is with you wherever you go.

Romans 8:38 - For I am persuaded that neither death, nor life, nor angels, nor principalities, nor things present, nor things to come, nor powers, nor height, nor depth, nor any other created thing, will be able to separate us from God's love which is in Christ Jesus our Lord.

One entire wall had pieces of paper stuck together to create a large poster that read:

Psalm 23 - Yahweh is my shepherd: I shall lack nothing. He makes me lie down in green pastures. He leads me beside still waters. He restores my soul. He guides me in the paths of righteousness for his name's sake. Even though I walk through the valley of the shadow of death, I will fear no evil; for you are with me. Your rod and your staff, they comfort me. You prepare a table before me in the presence of my enemies. You anoint my head with oil. My cup runs over. Surely goodness and loving kindness shall follow me all the days of my life, and I will dwell in Yahweh's house forever.

2.

Blessed are those who mourn, for they shall be comforted.

Juan Jose picked up his two-year-old niece into his arms as Angelina exclaimed her delight with his presence. He flew her around the room like a bird as he held her firmly in his strong arms.

"How are you my beautiful Angelina?" he said.

Angelina did indeed look angelic with her giant brown eyes and beautiful brown curly hair. Her radiant smile warmed Juan Jose's heart as he held her in front of his face and looked into her eyes as a mutual bond of love emanated between the two beings connecting each to the other.

Juan Jose counted, *"Uno, dos, tres, wheeeeee!"* and lifted Angelina high above his head holding her securely with his strong arms.

"Ten quidado, mi hermano," María cautioned Juan Jose to be careful with her daughter as she browned the pork on a skewer in the open fire with savory smells wafting over the room.

"No te preocupes," he said, assuring her not to worry.

As María tended to the *estufa* she was glad that the mission team from the United States had installed a galvanized chimney to take the smoke up through the roof from her clay stove on which she cooked the soup and pork for this evening's meal. She fondly remembered Jaime, the minister, who had come each year to their village and had first worked on latrines and water drainage with the *Americanos* and the next year they brought the chimneys and her eyes had stopped watering. She had almost stopped coughing herself to sleep at night.

She thought about her Bible that was presented to her by *Señora* Anita from the mission team. María's deepening faith made her life better. Even after losing her husband in the flooding river, she was able to cope and move on with her life and to be a loving mother for her darling Angelina. Each time she looked into those big beautiful brown eyes she remembered her husband Ernesto and saw his eyes through the near exact resemblance.

Juan Jose put Angelina onto the floor and picked up his old well-worn weathered guitar from the corner of the room. He played a Spanish love song he had learned from a man who owned a guitar in the neighboring village four miles away. Angelina loved to listen to the sweet music and she whirled about the floor dancing to the song, smiling and spinning happily.

María dipped the soup into the earthenware bowls and beckoned Juan Jose and Angelina to join her at the tiny table in the corner across from the stove. Juan Jose bowed his head and thanked God for their many blessings and for the strength to swing the sickle on this day that had passed into nighttime.

María said, "Did you notice how large Melci's tummy is with child? I pray that both she and the baby do fine."

Juan Jose said, "I pray that someday our valley will have a hospital with doctors to help when things go wrong."

"Yes, and to help all of the young children and adults who get sick and die," said María.

"I wish that the soon-to-be father had stayed to marry Melci," said Juan Jose.

"She will be better off without him."

"I pray the gospel will continue to spread in our valley and families will learn all of the truths found in the faith," avowed Juan Jose.

Angelina found the lack of attention being paid to her undesirable and emitted a loud wail followed by incomprehensible babble.

"Angelina, do you want your Tío Juan Jose to finish eating and play you another song on the guitar?" said Juan Jose.

Soon the happy sounds of Juan Jose's voice and the guitar echoed off the clay walls of María's *casa* until the dusk settled in. Without electricity, the village grew to darkness early as the candles were snuffed one by one. Juan Jose and María tucked Angelina into her small bed and said bedtime prayers from their knees beside her.

Juan Jose unrolled his mat and bedcovers onto the dirt floor alongside María's bed in the small room. The day's labor made sleep come easy. His nightly mantra of the opening sentence of the 23rd Psalm – The Lord is my shepherd – lasted only seven repetitions until he was fast asleep.

At first, Juan Jose thought he was dreaming when he was jolted awake by a piercing scream from a neighboring hut, the anguished female's cry breaking the silence of the night. He sat up on the floor long enough to gather his wits, jump into his blue jeans and bolt out of the door.

Melci screamed in a pitiful raw cry, "My babies, oh my poor *gemelos!*"

The twins were eleven weeks premature and the pitiful little babies, no more than a pound or two, were fighting for breaths of life. Without the help of a respirator they were battling to force enough oxygen into their tiny underdeveloped lungs. Melci clutched the small struggling forms to her breast and wailed and sobbed.

Juan Jose entered the room and pushed past the onlookers and gently knelt, kissed her forehead and assessed the situation.

He commanded Melci, "Keep them warm." Then he gently touched the struggling babies as he prayed aloud, "Holy Father, keep them breathing until I return."

Juan Jose jumped up shoving past the crowd and ran up the dirt road and across the large stones placed in the river. He thought prayerfully, if only I can reach the ranch with the missionaries quickly, and that a doctor is on a mission trip there.

After a mile, his lungs were aching for rest but he pushed on and ran even faster. The ground and occasional stone pounded his feet since he had not taken time to put on his only pair of shoes when he awakened to Melci's cries. The moonlight lit the way down the deeply rutted road as he rushed past a sleeping village for another mile. His lungs screamed to stop but he thought of the gasping twins and sprinted the final yards down the path to the guard shack just inside the ranch.

The guard drew his pistol as the crazy man pumping his arms approached running fast toward him without shoes.

"Alto!" he shouted, pointing his pistol at Juan Jose.

Juan Jose halted abruptly and gulped air explaining between breaths about the newborn twins in his village in need of a doctor. The guard swung open the gate and commanded Juan Jose to jump into his truck. A pediatrician from the United States happened to be at the ranch on a mission trip from her church in Austin, Texas and the guard knocked on the mahogany door of the women's dormitory shouting, *"Médica, médica, donde está la doctora?"*

Dr. Moss was awakened by the shouts and she quickly realized they were summoning her to duty as she strapped on her sandals. She was already dressed in green medical scrubs in which she was sleeping. Dr. Moss grabbed her medical bag and rushed to the truck. Juan Jose and the guard jumped in alongside her and the truck sped down the road. Juan Jose was glad that she spoke Spanish as he explained to her the tiny size of the twins and how he had told their mother Melci to keep them warm. He asked the doctor if she would join him in prayer for the babies as the truck raced down the road while trying to avoid the largest ruts.

Soon the truck rumbled into Juan Jose's village as he directed the guard toward Melci's little hut. Dr. Moss leapt from the vehicle and rushed into the tiny *casa*. The crowd of Melci's relatives and friends parted to let the doctor walk to the bed where Melci lay clutching her preemies, praying for them to keep breathing. The doctor exclaimed in Spanish that she was there to help try and save the twins. She asked for a blanket that she placed carefully inside her medical bag and then asked for Juan Jose and the guard to help carry Melci to the truck. She gently laid the twins inside the warm bag. As the guard and Melci settled into the cab of the truck, Dr. Moss and Juan Jose sat in the rear cab seat. Dr. Moss began to lift one and then the other and gently blow rescue breaths into the tiny mouths, alternating between the two of them as she forced oxygen into the two newborn brothers. At the same time she instructed Juan Jose to gently apply chest compressions on alternating babies. Like a well-orchestrated team, the two of them passed the babies back and forth after performing their life saving procedures.

Dr. Moss asked the guard to drive as fast as possible the two-and-a-half-hour trip out of the valley to the nearest town with a hospital. Juan Jose prayed for the babies while assisting Dr. Moss as they traveled the great distance to the hospital. He also prayed there would not be *banditos* along the road in the middle of the night looking for trouble. Melci prayed too, between sobs, as she hurt from both the fatigue of delivery and the worry for her babies. The trip seemed to take an eternity but they finally arrived and Dr. Moss gently carried the twins as the guard and Juan Jose located an old wheelchair and transported Melci into the hospital. The clock read 2:00 a.m.

Juan Jose sat exhausted in the hospital waiting room slumped in the small mahogany chair as he prayed for the babies whom Melci named Luis and Humberto. The room's silence made Juan Jose even sleepier, but he refused to slumber, as he knew his praying was paramount. Two hours passed when Dr. Moss finally came into the room and whispered to Juan Jose that the twins were alive. She was surprised to find the hospital equipped with twenty-year-old incubators and an even older ventilator for treating respiratory distress syndrome, but the equipment was working to save the twins' lives.

Dr. Moss, Juan Jose and the guard climbed into the truck and started the trek back to Juan Jose's village and to the ranch. Juan Jose tried to stay awake but his eyes shut tight from exhaustion from a hard day's work and an even harder night's journey. The truck bumped along the rutted road leading into the valley and Juan Jose's head jerked awake every few minutes with each hard bump from the back cab seat. Finally, at 6:30 a.m. the truck rumbled into the village and Juan Jose thanked Dr. Moss for saving the babies.

"Muchas gracias y vaya con Dios," he said with much appreciation and admiration. For the first time, he studied the doctor's face and peered into her stunningly beautiful blue eyes. Her long blond hair, even though disheveled from the long night, framed her beautiful silky face. In a word, she was the most beautiful woman Juan Jose had ever seen. She stared back at Juan Jose and her perfect thick pink

lips curled into a heartwarming smile.

"*El gusto es mío,*" she said with "the pleasure is mine."

Juan Jose sensed her keen intelligence and was attracted to this woman who seemed so smart and beautiful. He wondered how she had become so well-educated with the opportunity to become a doctor.

"*Buenos noches,* I mean *buenos días,*" Juan Jose said to Dr. Moss as the first rooster crowed his good morning salute to the world. As the truck pulled away, Juan Jose went back to his hut and stoked a fire to boil water for the fresh coffee beans he had crushed with a rock the day before. With his hot steaming cup in hand he sipped and began his morning ritual of prayers. Perhaps it was the excitement of the night now diminished to silence or his aching body in need of sleep rather than the stimulation of the caffeine, but Juan Jose became very emotional in his prayers. He wept for the twins who had almost died.

If only we had a hospital in our valley, he cried to himself and to God. Then he cried for Melci, the young mother who was alone and without the companionship and love from the father of the babies. He cried for the children in the valley who would be hungry on this day. He cried for the children who were sick and in need of medical care. Lastly he cried for his own evil thoughts each day that invaded his mind and kept him from being pure. Juan Jose mourned his sins and the sins of the valley. The only thing that pulled him out of his deep melancholy was the thought of the beautiful smiling lips of Dr. Moss and how she had worked through the night to save Luis and Humberto.

3.

Blessed are the gentle,
for they shall inherit the earth.

Juan Jose started the long walk toward work. He knew this would be a tough day because of his lack of sleep from the long travel to the hospital in helping to save the twins' lives during the night.

The morning fog hung in the valley like a white cotton gown on a clothesline and obscured Juan Jose's vision of the mountains. He walked determinedly down the uneven road, jumping over the small potholes in the earth and stepping around the deep ruts made from tires, rain and mud. He carried his sickle in his right hand playing a game by flipping it ahead of him twice in the air and then catching the handle perfectly with his left hand. Then he tossed it with his left hand and after two perfect turns in the air he would catch it in his right hand all the while keeping the same pace on the road and hopping over the potholes. It made the time pass quickly and soon he was walking toward the job foreman Tim.

Tim Bigelow stood in the field like a tall volcano about to erupt because of his head pounding from the large quantity of fermented liquor that he had consumed in the night. He had learned from the locals to ferment the jicaro tree pulp. Tim gave Juan Jose a scornful look as he told Juan Jose to leave his sickle on the ground.

"*El jefe* Carlos wants to try you at cutting down trees with the chainsaw, so it's your lucky day, slacker. You're to head up to the forest, and *pronto!*"

"*Por favor,* I will be pleased to cut the fields but will not go into the old-growth pine forest and cut trees illegally."

"You will do what I say, or you can pick up your sickle and go home."

"*Señor*, please understand that I do not wish to lose my job, but neither can I help to destroy our forest."

"Get out of my sight, you wretch! You're fired!"

Tim swung his large hand suddenly and backhanded Juan Jose across his face. The sudden movement caught Juan Jose off guard and the blow cracked his lip, splitting it against his upper teeth, and the red blood poured forth from his stinging lip. He tasted the blood and spat it out making splotches of red on the green grass beneath. Juan Jose backed away and stared at Tim who stood on his sickle with his giant brown worn boot. Juan Jose knew he could take Tim in a fight. His agility and speed could easily topple the giant.

Juan Jose stared at the enormous man and looked into his eyes for a full minute. Tim lifted his foot off the sickle and backed away after taking a machete from the scabbard attached to his belt. Juan Jose watched him warily as he waited until Tim was backed well away and then he bent to pick up his sickle and turned away quickly to make a declaration he was not going to fight, but alertly listening for any rush of footsteps behind him for fear that Tim might attack.

None came. Juan Jose's body ached from his lack of sleep and from bouncing down the roads to the hospital the previous night and his mouth continued to burn in pain. Maybe on another day, he would have tried to find the landowner to plead his case. Today, he simply prayed to God to strengthen and lead him, picked up his sickle and headed back down the road.

"*Dios*, I do not know how I will find work but I will put my trust in You. Lead me where You want me to go. Light my path so that I can walk with Your Son and glorify You. I pray that *Señor* Tim might find You and find love in his heart instead of darkness. In the name of Your Holy Son I pray. Amen."

Juan Jose knew that he needed to refresh himself and meditate and pray. He was not far from the waterfall and he began a fast pace to walk the three miles to the cascading water. He waved at the children playing in their small yards amongst the chickens and pigs as he walked past the small white adobe houses. Huge smiles, large brown eyes and friendly waves greeted him as he traversed to the waterfall. Juan Jose hopped over the small brook and began the slight climb upwards. He heard the crisp sound of the tumbling stream and soon stood on the cliff looking down at the lush green fern-lined pool formed from the last drop-off of fifteen feet of white gushing water. He worked his way down the narrow path, stepping onto the last large gray stone and then leaping across the torrent. He thought of the vastness of the water pouring from high in the mountains and feeding the plants of the valley and likened it to God's source of goodness that flows into the hearts of believers. A large log wedged between boulders made an inviting seat as he worked his way onto the log and turned to his left to meditate with his eyes fixed on the pouring waters crashing into the pool.

Juan Jose began to think and pray, "Almighty *Dios*, I know that You will be with me as I struggle through the challenge of finding work. I pray that whatever I do, it would be for Your glory. Forgive me for my bad feelings toward *Señor* Tim and I pray that he would be changed and someday walk in Your light. I pray for my village and our valley and for Melci's babies. Thank you for Your grace that pours from the heavens and steadies us in Your word. Now, I will listen for Your voice. I empty myself so that I may be filled with Your Holy Spirit. Help me to be still and know that You are God."

Juan Jose sat for more than an hour staring into the swirling water. He finally heard an inner voice telling him to go back to his village. He jumped into the natural pool, ice-like cold shocking his body as he refreshed himself and then strode purposefully toward home.

As he approached the common ground in the village where the missionaries had built the small pole barn church, he heard a great commotion. He noticed the flatbed diesel truck from the mission ranch parked alongside the church and knew that the mission team was on the premises. He sprinted to the church when he saw the colorful yellow bandana wrapped around the head of the person who had taught him the gospel and baptized him in the river.

"Jaime!" he exclaimed joyously while rushing to his arms for a warm embrace. *"Cómo estás, mí amigo?"*

"Muy bien. Muy bien. It is so good to see you my friend. What has it been? A year at least, since I went back to the U.S., but now I have returned to this magnificent valley to be with all of you wonderful people."

Juan Jose couldn't help but notice the dazzling blonde hair of Dr. Moss who was on her hands and knees under the church overhang on the concrete patio playing with the children. She was making noises like a pig and then chasing the children around a circle as they squealed with delight.

The other missionaries were opening boxes of cookies for the children and singing songs while a talented female guitar player strummed the joyful music and sang beautifully.

Juan Jose was grateful for Jaime and his church in the U.S. who had adopted their village and had assisted the villagers in making all of the improvements and had even taught their women to sew on hand turned spindle sewing machines. The church from Texas had also sent teachers and educators every year who had helped train the Honduran teachers and provided many school supplies. Construction teams had built kinder furniture for the students, making chairs and desks from plywood as well as bookcases and larger teachers' chairs and desks. Best of all, the Americans had built the church building on one of their trips which was also used as a small community center for celebrations such as today.

Dr. Moss turned her head from the floor and noticed Juan Jose talking to Jaime. She stood up and walked over to the two of them and said in fluent Spanish, "This is the man I told you about who saved the twins last night."

"No, *Doctora*. You are the one who saved the twins," said Juan Jose.

"Let's say it was a team effort," she said and smiled another beautiful smile like the night before that Juan Jose caringly remembered. Her brilliant white teeth were perfect. Juan Jose knew he would never forget that smile or her kind voice.

Jaime said, "I should have known it was you my friend, whom Dr. Julie told me ran through the night to save the twins."

Juan Jose made a mental note that the beautiful woman's first name was Julie as he said meekly, "It was nothing."

The female guitar player named Karen from the mission team walked over to where they were standing and said, "Please translate for me Jaime. Juan Jose, I understand that you play the guitar. Please, we would be honored if you take it and play for us."

Jaime translated and Juan Jose smiled and reached

forward for the guitar. Such a beautiful instrument this was – a handcrafted guitar made in Austin, Texas. The sound was magnificent as Juan Jose plucked the strings skillfully and sang a song by native Honduran Guillermo Anderson called *"En Mi País."*

As Juan Jose sang, his eyes connected with Dr. Julie several times as he serenaded and played the amazing guitar. The instrument and Juan Jose's voice seemed to be perfectly tuned as his sweet playing and singing even captivated the attention of the children as they shushed to listen to the beautiful music, spellbound by the marvelous sound.

When Juan Jose finished, Dr. Julie not only applauded loudly with the rest, but she stepped over closer and draped her arm over his shoulder and lightly squeezed him. Her touch sent warmth all through his body and he thanked her for the recognition saying, "I'm glad you liked the song and my guitar playing. Music brings joy to my heart and is a gift from God."

Julie said, "I love music. Sometimes it brings me very close to God and this was one of those times."

"Gracias," said Juan Jose humbly as he handed the instrument back to the missionary named Karen.

The children resumed playing games with Dr. Julie as Jaime walked over to the flatbed truck and opened the cab pulling out his bag of golf clubs. Jaime walked back to the crowd and interrupted saying, "I brought something for you villagers to try. Have you ever seen a golf club?"

He walked over to the grassy area, unzipped a pocket on the bag and took out what looked like a tiny soccer ball and placed it carefully sitting up in the grass. He then drew his seven-iron from the bag.

Juan Jose looked curiously at the gray stick with a shiny small blade on one end and some kind of padding wrapped around the other end. Several of the villagers gathered around to see what was about to happen as Jaime explained how to place their fingers on the club.

"What does it do?" Juan Jose said.

"It is used to play the finest game in the world."

"I have never seen one in a *fútbol* game," said Juan Jose.

"Yes, yes, *fútbol* is a fine game. But this game called golf is played with the skill of one instead of the skill of many. A golfer must also master the earth and the weather, as well as his opponents, to win," Jaime said very seriously, his green eyes dazzling with intent. "But most of all, a golfer must master himself and overcome his own mind to concentrate and win."

Juan Jose looked down at the small ball sitting in the grass. He bent over and picked it up to examine it carefully. It was so tiny. He thought that it must be a soccer ball made for roosters to play with, if you could teach animals to play. He turned it over in his hands and noticed the hardness and dimples. Juan Jose thought about how it would hurt his foot to kick the tiny hard ball, and a rooster's as well. As he held the small orb in his hand, Juan Jose sensed that there was a greater power inside the hard shell – something waiting to be released like a chicken ready to hatch. He reached out toward Jaime holding the ball nestled in his palm.

As Jaime took the golf ball from Juan Jose's hand he said, "You take this golf ball and strike it with the golf club. The idea is to make it go straight at your target along your chosen flight. I know it sounds simple, but it is very difficult to accomplish consistently."

Jaime placed the small white *bola* onto a tuft of grass and gripped the golf club with both hands. The club moved back around him slowly as Jaime turned his back and coiled like a spring. Then he unleashed his coiled power back around with a fluid motion as the shiny silver blade hit the ball. The ball made a clicking sound upon impact and sped upward, a small white dot rising toward the blue sky.

Juan Jose watched in amazement. Suddenly the ball began to turn to the right, losing momentum, falling from the sky as Jaime said loudly, "Ding, dangit. I sliced that one!"

Juan Jose noticed Jaime was no longer smiling and his brow was raised. He had been transformed into an angrier person than one minute before. Juan Jose wondered what power this thing called golf has over a person's emotions.

Jaime reached into the golf bag and set another ball upon another tuft of grass. Juan Jose noticed that the blade had removed the grass neatly away from where he had hit before.

"You try it," Jaime said as he passed the golf club to one of the villagers named Raul. Raul was twenty years old and was short and thin. His tattered pants made him look like a scarecrow whose stuffing had fallen out. He wore an old t-shirt that had been sent over as a hand-me-down from the U.S. that read, "Karl's Crispy Chicken – where it doesn't matter which came first – the chicken or the egg!"

Jaime instructed him how to hold the club with what he referred to as the golf grip. He told him to grip the club like he was holding a baby bird that he didn't want to hurt nor want the bird to get away from his hands. He showed him how to address the ball – the stance is what he called this ready position.

Raul turned awkwardly and swung with his arms and hands flailing downward toward the ball while his body lifted up ever so slightly but enough to alter the club's plane causing him to miss striking the ball entirely.

The group of boys and men gathered around laughed loudly at Raul's expense. Raul tried once more and missed and the laughter erupted again.

Next, Lucas, who was the oldest man amongst them being sixty-one years old, gripped the club and stepped up addressing the ball. He turned ever so slightly but brought his hands and club high up into the air, descending straight down as if killing a snake with a shovel. The golf ball was topped into the ground and thudded forward about six inches. Again, laughter erupted from the onlookers and Raul especially enjoyed the joke at the expense of someone other than himself.

Another villager named Roberto took the seven-iron and moved the club back around his body in a flat manner and managed to strike the ball severely on the outside farthest from him, causing the ball to spin viciously and slicing into the adjacent field off to the right. The group applauded his effort at moving the ball.

Jaime said, "That's what everyone does when they first start out, coming outside to in and slicing the ball. Who's next?"

Juan Jose stepped forward and carefully placed the club into his hands folding his fingers securely around it until his hands felt like a single unit. The great Ben Hogan would have pointed to his hands and declared his grip fundamentally sound.

Jaime said, "Juan Jose, you look so relaxed. You look like a natural golfer. There is no tension in your arms or shoulders and this will free you to make a good turn."

Juan Jose cannot explain what happened next because his muscles simply took over and his mind went blank. Just as he had done for ten years in the fields swinging the sickle to and fro, he knew only that he wanted to remove the grass in the neat little swatch like Jaime had done. He heard a loud *swoosh* as the club cut through the wind and then he felt the *click* as the ball launched from the impact of the blade. He quickly found the ball in his sight as his head came about and his hands finished high around the back left side of his neck. Words do not do justice to the feeling Juan Jose had as he watched the white golf ball rocket into the blue sky. He could not believe that the stick with a shiny silver blade had shot the ball like a gun shoots a bullet into the air.

"Great, Scott!" Jaime exclaimed as the crowd of men erupted into loud applause and whistling. "You must have hit that seven-iron 190 yards. Straight as an arrow, it was. Perfect. Did you see the way it rose up to a great height and then dropped to the earth like a dove that's been shot at the top of its flight?"

Juan Jose noticed the straight swath of brown dirt where the blade had passed and removed the grass. This pleased him more than the excitement of Jaime.

"You've got to try this club," Jaime said, as he reached into the funny bag and handed him another tool. "This is called a two-iron."

Juan Jose noticed immediately that the length was several centimeters longer. The shiny blade was not angled as much. He thought about how this slight slant would cause the ball to go farther and with less height than the other club. He asked Jaime to hit first so that he could notice any differences.

Jaime explained, "One of the harder clubs in the bag to hit, this one is. I'll give it a try but my percentage is not very good. I would use a hybrid on the course instead of a two-iron."

He stood a little farther from the ball because of the added length. The grip looked the same and everything else was similar. As the clubhead descended into the ball everyone heard a sharp noisy *crack!* as the *bola* left the blade. The ball shot left of center and never rose above a couple of meters from the ground. It turned farther left and jumped into the banana grove tearing through the vibrant green leaves.

Juan Jose noticed that the cut grass from the blade of the club pointed to the right.

"Geeze, Louise!" Jaime cried out in anguish. "I usually slice the ball, but that was a full-blown hook. That's the first time I've hit a banana with a hook," he chuckled to himself, but no one else understood the double meaning joke referring to slices and hooks. "Here, you try it. I told you that I couldn't hit a two-iron."

Once again Juan Jose stood over the ball and thought of nothing. He shifted his weight and the club back and then forth with a rhythm that matched life itself – the ebb and flow of the tide, the inhale and exhale of breath, the rise and fall of the rain filled river, the light and dark of a day. For him, the swing was easy and required no thought. *Swoosh! Click!* The ball shot forth from the earth tearing through the air towards the heavens. He looked at the clump of cropped grass that flew away from the earth several yards ahead and in line with the path of the ball and then he found the white ball zooming forward into the sky. This shiny blade was indeed his club of choice for cutting out grass.

"Wow!" Jaime yelled as the group applauded loudly. "Look at that ball flight!"

On and on the ball traveled until Juan Jose squinted trying to follow its flight in the great distance. He was unable to find proper words to describe his feeling. Juan Jose knew he was a simple man and perhaps 'joy' was the best description he could say for what had just happened.

How can it be that this white ball and bladed stick can make me feel the same as when I hold my sister's daughter Angelina and she smiles at me? Perhaps there is a spirit inside the ball that provides joy for being released when the blade strikes the ball. Perhaps the spirit is only released when the ball is struck perfectly.

He certainly noticed that Jaime was not finding any joy from his hits. Juan Jose vowed to himself to always swing in such a way to release the spirit of joy from the golf ball as his mind rippled thoughts like rocks dropped into a still pond.

Juan Jose looked around and noticed the entire village and missionaries had stopped their raucous reunion and begun to crowd toward him to see what was happening. Juan Jose caught the eye of Dr. Julie whose warm smile toward him made him think of the simple word 'joy' again. He grinned back at her and then shyly turned away.

Jaime said, "This is a pitching wedge. See how close you can land a ball to that palm tree over there near the soccer field."

Juan Jose looked at the steep angle of the blade and knew instinctively that the ball would travel high into the air. He took aim on the palm and pictured the ball landing into the center of the palm leaves at the top of the tree. Again his rhythm matched a cadence deep within his soul, embedded within from swinging the sickle for many years, as the simple tick tock of his golf swing struck the ball perfectly as it skyrocketed upward. A hundred and ten sets of eyes followed the flight of the small white orb as it soared into the sky and then dropped dead center of the palm leaves at the top of the tree.

"Bueno, muy bueno!" the crowd cheered and clapped for the incredible feat they had just witnessed.

Jaime's heart beat rapidly as he pondered what he had just discovered about Juan Jose in this remote village in Central Honduras in the beauty of the Agalta Valley. He knew he must test Juan Jose's remarkable natural skill against an opponent on a golf course. The closest place to play golf would be The Tegucigalpa Green Tee Club, about seven hours away.

Dr. Julie stepped closer to speak to Jaime. "Can you believe that swing? My father taught me to play golf when I was ten and in all my years I have never witnessed a swing so smooth and pure." Chills flowed up her spine as she stated this fact.

Juan Jose did not understand her English but knew she was speaking about him. He sensed that somehow the simple act of hitting the golf ball had astonished the Americans and he wondered why all the attention for something as easy as this.

Jaime said to him, "Juan Jose, God has given you a gift and we must go to Tegucigalpa in the morning to try it on a golf course. I will pay you for the wages you will miss by not working tomorrow. Is this acceptable to you?"

Juan Jose said, "I was fired from my job today for refusing to cut trees in our old-growth pine forest and now, you have given me an opportunity to earn wages tomorrow. My faith is in things not seen and hope in tomorrow. I will be honored to accompany you to the city, although I've never been farther than Juticalpa."

Jaime loaded his golf clubs back into the truck and the missionaries stepped up into the big diesel, being assisted by one of the men who guided their feet into the metal step bracket while another pulled them up into the bed of the truck reaching out and grasping the ladies' hands. Dr. Julie made a point of touching Juan Jose on his shoulder as she passed by him waving *adiós*.

Later that night, Juan Jose played his guitar for Angelina and his sister María. As he lay down on his bed he fell asleep saying his prayers, thanking God for the day, thanking God for the missionaries, thanking God for the wages he would be paid by Jaime and thanking God for the pretty doctor who had saved Melci's twins.

Bump, bump, bump! Jaime and Juan Jose traveled the next morning over rain washed jutted roads until they left the Agalta Valley and reached the main highway that goes to Tegucigalpa. About three hours after starting their journey they arrived at a bakery and stopped for a delicious homemade cookie and cola beverage. They drove onward until reaching the city and Juan Jose was amazed at the mass of humanity living in small wooden buildings, one on top of the other, reaching all the way up the hills. The people, streets and cars overwhelmed his mind and his sense of sight was like a child coloring madly with crayons. He had never imagined, from living within the peacefulness of his village, that such a busy place existed.

Jaime said, "We will find you some proper clothes for golfing and also buy you some golf shoes in the pro shop. Then we will go to the course and you and I will play a round of golf after I show you how to putt."

Juan Jose already missed his village and was afraid of the honking horns, screeching tires and masses of people walking faster than he had ever seen people walking – like they had to be somewhere immediately and would not see tomorrow.

How strange it must be to be in such a hurry, he thought to himself. Perhaps all of these people walking so fast are racing the present, trying to beat tomorrow, and so they must hurry along cheating the time of the moment. He thought of how they should walk slower, enjoying the day and noticing the things that count in life, like the green tree-topped mountains that form the valley, the tall ceiba trees with roots as large as elephants angled like sails sticking into the ground, the hibiscus that bloom bright colors, the river that pushes cool waters through the valley, their families and friends and especially following at a steady pace along the path of God's choosing. Strangely the bustle of the city seemed to have swallowed many of these things or hidden them from Juan Jose's view.

Jaime drove the road that ascended to the hills beyond the city and Juan Jose looked behind, down at all of the buildings as they wound around the mountain and left the capital of Honduras. About thirty kilometers away they turned onto a road that led to the golf course. The beautiful green grass reminded him of home because the flowers, the trees and the stream of water they crossed looked so peaceful. He began to feel better immediately and didn't care if he ever saw the big city again. Juan Jose noticed that the green grass was cut at three different levels. There were large circle-like areas with the closest cut grass he had ever seen. Jaime called them greens and said that this was the area they would be trying to send their balls to and from those areas they would putt. He didn't understand the word putt although, as Jaime explained the idea of rolling the ball into a hole in the green, Juan Jose began to visualize the ball dropping from the surface like an animal scurrying into its home in the earth.

Jaime parked the car and Juan Jose followed him into a magnificent building through large mahogany doors with a brass sign that read Pro Shop. One section of the room had more clothes than Juan Jose had ever seen in one place. Racks of colorful shirts hung from metal rods. He looked to the other side of the room and saw new shiny golf clubs all in a line like soldiers in a row waiting to march. An old man with many hard lines across his face but with a peaceful look that peeked through the wrinkles like the sunshine filtering through the trees greeted Jaime warmly. Jaime explained to the old man that Juan Jose needed to be outfitted for a round of golf.

The friendly old Honduran asked him, "What size shirt do you wear?"

Jaime told him, "Juan Jose is a small man but has a big heart in case that matters."

The old man chuckled to himself and had Juan Jose try on several of the brightly colored knit shirts. Never in his life had Juan Jose seen anything as new and fancy as these colorful shirts. He had always worn t-shirts sent by missionaries to his valley to help clothe the poor.

Next, the old man found a pair of khaki colored pants that were brand new and showed Juan Jose where to change in the men's locker room. The transformation was amazing. Juan Jose almost looked like a golfer except for his worn shoes. Jaime told him to remove them, put on the socks he handed him and try on the funny shoes with rubber bumps on the bottom. Jaime said they were called spikes and would keep his feet from slipping on the course.

Jaime paid the old man and led Juan Jose out to the putting green. Juan Jose noticed all of the little holes and poles with colorful yellow flags. Jaime told him to hold his putter and ball and he would check them in for the golf round, get their caddies arranged and rent Juan Jose a set of clubs.

Juan Jose bent over and felt the smooth grass. He noticed the tiny grasses matted together and saw that the grain grew in a certain direction. It looked shinier when he looked at it from different angles and from different directions. He noticed the different contours and imagined his valley with its rolling hills and green mountains. Jaime returned with another bag full of clubs. He handed Juan Jose the putter from the bag while taking back his own and began to explain.

"The grip is different for this one, my friend," he said, as he aligned his thumbs down the middle of the shaft and used all ten fingers on the club. "The stroke is also different – like a pendulum swinging back and forth without involving your wrists."

Juan Jose observed the grip as Jaime's right hand held the putter shaft across the lifeline of his palm. He had never seen a pendulum but he observed Jaime's motion and took his grip on the putter. The club felt like an extension of his arms and hands and he was enthusiastic to try to make the ball go into the hole.

Jaime stood behind his ball and squatted and peered at both his ball and the hole. He explained that he was reading the break. Then he aligned himself alongside the ball. Juan Jose noticed that his alignment was about two centimeters different from where he would have aimed because of the slope of the green. Jaime stroked the ball and it missed the hole on the downside and rolled a few feet past the cup.

"Don't do what I did," he said tersely. "I should have started the ball up higher to account for more break."

Juan Jose placed his ball on the beautiful green grass. He squatted as Jaime had done and picked and drew an imaginary line from the ball, curving into the hole. He looked at the spot above the hole where he was aiming, back at the hole and then back down at the ball. Then he saw the hole in his mind and they became connected by the path from which his ball was about to travel. His hands became the link from ball to hole and they moved fluidly back and through the ball as he pictured the ball falling into the opening. He looked up after stroking the ball and followed the ball rolling perfectly along his intended route into the cup. As it disappeared from the green he heard a strange echoing as the ball plopped into the hole. He found this sound to be pleasing and knew that he wanted to hear this noise after each putting stroke. This resonance became his motivation for making the putt as he thought about how it completed that moment's destiny for the ball.

"Great putt! You have great touch and a feel for putting as well as shot making. Now try a long one. That hole way over there."

Juan Jose surveyed the green once again and noticed two hills rising between him and the hole. He thought about the river back home and how it flows over the sloped banks and he visualized water flowing over the green and running with the shape. He chose a spot to putt to so that the ball would run down the slope and flow into the hole. He also observed the grain of the grass pointing back at him. He instinctively knew that the grass would slow his putt as the tiny mesh increased friction on the ball instead of reducing friction like putts with-the-grain. Once again he looked to the line where he had chosen to putt and aligned the putter blade to send the ball along this path. He looked at the hole for an instant and became connected before concentrating once more on the spot he wanted to putt the ball just before the downward slope. Keeping his head perfectly still so he would hit the exact spot on the ball intended, Juan Jose stroked it smoothly and awaited that marvelous sound. The ball rose through the first hill and then turned left as he had anticipated with his water visualization. Then the ball just made the top of the second bank and turned right sloping downward as he had envisioned, sending it rolling towards the hole. *Plop, echo,* the ball sounded out as it reached the destination and bounced a couple of times in the hard plastic cup.

"Amazing!" was all Jaime could say, as if he didn't expect the ball to go into the cup.

Juan Jose noticed the colorful flowers alongside the clubhouse and thought about the blooming bromeliads in the trees back home. He liked the game already because it used nature as its setting and he found great tranquility at the golf course.

Jaime explained to Juan Jose about who a caddie is and how he would carry Juan Jose's bag and give advice on the course as he finished saying, "The caddies are waiting. Are you ready to play?"

Juan Jose said, "Yes, I think that I will like this game you call golf."

Jaime introduced Juan Jose to Luis and Humberto. Juan Jose immediately thought of the strange coincidence that these were the names of Melci's new babies. The young caddies were in their teens and although they wore the white jumpsuit of the club, Jaime told Juan Jose that they were from poor families that lived nearby. Luis picked up Juan Jose's bag and the four of them walked toward the rectangular area of closely cropped green grass. Jaime showed Juan Jose the first tee and instructed him how to read the map on the scorecard to see the bend of the fairway before straightening to the hole. He told Juan Jose to swing the same way as he had with the irons. Juan Jose looked down at the enormous titanium head and thought to himself how easy it would be to make solid contact in the center of the club. He couldn't believe how light the club felt in his hands.

"Straight and long always works with the driver," Jaime said. "Of course if you can make an inside-out-swing and hit the ball here," he said pointing to a dimple on the ball in the quadrant closest to his back foot and inside an imaginary line drawn from the center of the ball toward the target "it will draw and travel a great distance farther."

Juan Jose noted the spot he showed him and thought about angling his feet, legs and shoulders to just slightly face right of the target so that he could try one of these shots that Jaime called a draw.

Jaime stood for a long time over his ball thinking, as if trying to will the ball to go straight, and then swung back and through the ball. He sliced it off into the grove of trees about 190 yards to the right.

"Terrible way to start," he said with a frown. "And the hole doglegs left. That's why I was explaining a draw shot to you. Hope, you've better luck than me, my friend."

Juan Jose carefully placed the small wooden peg into the earth with the ball positioned for just the right height as Jaime had instructed. He took his grip and aligned his body slightly right for the draw. He looked down the fairway, many yards away, where it started to turn left and envisioned his ball following that turn. Juan Jose relaxed his mind and body and then swung as if he were cutting through a dense jungle groundcover with his sickle with a rhythm that would allow him to swing the same all day in the hot sun. He heard a wonderful metallic pinging sound as the ball shot off the tee. The ball whizzed down the fairway and began its turn toward the left. Juan Jose couldn't believe how far it went, nor could Luis, Humberto or Jaime.

"Incredible," Luis said. "Has to be 325 plus yards. I'll bet you only need a wedge to reach the green."

Juan Jose began to feel sorry for Jaime who seemed to try so hard and could not even come close to his own early success with the golfclubs. Humberto found Jaime's ball amongst the trees and Jaime hit a low shot out of the woods back onto the fairway by playing the ball farther back toward his right foot. Juan Jose made a mental note of the ball positioning and the shot he referred to as a punch. Next, Jaime chose a three-wood as he was still 200 yards away from the green. His ball turned slightly right and so it landed well right of the hole in a large pit. Juan Jose noted that Jaime called this a sand trap and acted like it was a dreadful thing to be in.

Juan Jose was only 100 yards from the hole, so Luis suggested using the lob wedge because he had hit his drive so far. Juan Jose stood much closer to the ball with this club and knew from the angle of the iron that it would sail the ball very high into the sky, like the wedge he had hit at the village yesterday, only this club would send it even higher. He looked at the flag sticking out of the hole and thought about landing the ball to hit as near the cup as possible. Once again, the hole and his mind became linked. Both were empty, awaiting fulfillment from the swing. He turned back and then through, letting his swing find the golf ball through its natural motion while focused on the joy of the swing and not the stillness of the ball before impact. He watched as the white dot ascended rapidly into the sky. Up, up, up it carried and then dropped straight toward the flagstick. As he and Luis approached the green he noticed the ball rested about two feet in front of the cup. As Luis repaired the ball mark he showed Juan Jose that it had landed only an inch or two from the cup. Juan Jose noticed how it had backed up from the landing spot. From now on

I must hit slightly above the cup and back it into the hole, he thought to himself.

Jaime walked into the sand trap and explained to Juan Jose how to use a sand wedge by opening the face and hitting into the sand behind the ball and spraying the sand to move the ball from underneath. He must have had a lot of practice at this kind of shot because he flew the ball out very nicely and it rolled to within five feet of the hole. Juan Jose decided that he would prefer not to have to learn how to hit this shot and with all of that pretty green grass he did not see any point in hitting his ball into the sand. Humberto raked the trap and Juan Jose thought to himself that it looked more fun to rake than to make the shot from the sand.

Jaime explained that the ball farthest from the cup must go first. He looked over his five-foot putt and then stroked the ball. It started toward the center of the cup but then broke slightly right and rolled around the circumference of the cup staying out of the hole. He walked to his ball sitting inches from the cup.

"Can I tap in?"

"I think you can make the putt," Juan Jose said.

He said, "No, I am asking your permission to let me tap in since you are now farthest from the hole, but I would like to finish if you will allow me."

"*Sí.* Tap in. *No problema,*" Juan Jose said.

After Jaime retrieved his successful tap-in from the cup, Juan Jose looked over the short distance between his ball and the hole. He decided to stroke the ball to hit the center of the cup and to hit it with enough speed to not have a chance to get caught in the break of the slight left-to-right slope. Again, he concentrated on the hole and saw the ball hitting the back of the cup dead center in his mind and then with his hands linked to his arms and shoulders he looked down at the ball and made it happen. The plopping echo sound of the ball bouncing around the bottom of the cup made him feel happy.

"Well done, my friend," Jaime said as he patted him on the back. "That's a birdie for you and a double bogey for me. A birdie is one stroke fewer than the established par for the hole and a bogey is one more stroke than par, so my double bogey means I scored a six and you scored a three."

Juan Jose didn't understand why he was explaining the bogey and double bogey language to him since he only intended to make birdies the rest of the day. Juan Jose thought, I am a simple man and threes are easier to add up in my mind than fives and sixes so a low number is not only desirable but necessary.

Jaime explained that the next hole was a par five dogleg right, further explaining how dogleg meant the bend of the fairway from tee box to green. He showed Juan Jose the bend on the layout printed on the scorecard and how the small lake of water protected the front side of the green.

Jaime said, "Your birdie has the honors and you are to lead the way on the next tee box."

As Juan Jose positioned his ball on the tee he thought about the little picture on the scorecard of this hole and about how it turned right, way down the fairway for the dogleg as Jaime had called it. He thought about Jaime's swing that always seemed to come outside in and make the ball go too far right. He decided to move his legs in his alignment to the ball slightly to the left so that he could try to make the ball turn right down the fairway by striking it ever so slightly to the right of center this time. Juan Jose turned and swung and the ball made that crisp pinging sound off the driver clubface once again. Rapidly it traveled down the fairway and began to turn right this time and disappeared around the dogleg out of their vision from the tee box.

"Muy bien. Es perfectamente!" exclaimed Luis.

"How did the ball turn so precisely?" said Jaime.

Juan Jose said, "I notice the little things that make a big difference. A slight move hugely changes the outcome."

"Yes, I know what you mean – that the small differences in the way the ball is struck makes the ball fly differently, but I am unable to change my swing in such small ways."

"One must consider the change, then forget with the mind and give it over to the body in order to complete the task," Juan Jose tried to explain. He sensed that the blanking of his mind and the taking over of his muscles was important in making the shots.

Jaime teed up his ball and swung better this time with the ball starting left and turning only slightly right. Juan Jose estimated that Jaime's ball was about seventy yards less down the fairway than his, since Jaime's ball was before the right turn and his was well into the turn. Jaime's next shot was a three-wood and the ball sailed left to right and seemed to disappear on the right side of the dogleg.

Juan Jose noticed the flag way off in the distance and estimated the green to be about the same distance he had hit the two-iron on the ranch. Luis told him he was 249 yards away. He would have to carry the water and he asked Luis for the two-iron so he could hit the ball over the water and onto the green. He aimed straight for the green and thought about the flag and the hole beneath. *Swoosh, click,* the club sounded as the ball sailed high into the sky. Juan Jose was confident it had landed on the green but they were too far away to see.

Jaime found his ball in the deeper cut of grass that he called the rough. He was still about 170 yards away and he chose his four-iron to strike the ball. The ball made an ugly sound and sped along the ground toward the lake. Jaime mumbled something to himself and made a slight kicking motion at the ground as if knocking some invisible animal in the head with his foot. Once again, Juan Jose felt sorry for his friend and wished that Jaime's shots would be more like his own, finding great joy in the swing.

Jaime dropped a new ball from the side of the water where the ball went in and explained to Juan Jose the penalty stroke for a lost ball in a water hazard. Juan Jose determined at that moment not to hit balls into water since a penalty stroke was undesirable, but more importantly, he knew it was wasteful and costly to send a perfectly good golf ball into the depths of a lake.

Jaime hit a nine-iron over the water safely onto the green but his ball was well long of the hole. Juan Jose noticed that his own ball rested twenty feet past the hole and he made a mental note that in the future to use his three-iron from 229 meters out to hit short of the cup and let it run up to the hole.

Juan Jose liked the way the game of golf was not only exercising his mind between the shots but also how the natural beauty of the course gave him serenity. He also realized how important it was to stop the mind exercise in making the shot and to just be. Juan Jose knew that part of Jaime's problem was his inability to stop his thoughts as he was making the swing. He could tell by the long amount of time that he stood over a ball before swinging that Jaime's mind was actively stalling a good swing.

Jaime explained to Juan Jose about an eagle being one stroke less than a birdie and very difficult and rare except for professional golfers who could eagle par fives from time to time or get lucky with an iron approach going in on a par four hole. Jaime's ball was beyond Juan Jose's and he squatted to read the break. Juan Jose could see a large left-to-right break and knew that Jaime would have to play the ball about five feet up from the cup to make this treacherous putt. As he stroked the ball, Juan Jose noticed the path being too low and the speed was too fast as well. The ball raced by a foot below the cup and rolled to a stop about eight feet away.

Juan Jose read the green from his ball's position and noticed even more break than Jaime's. He thought about how the ball would need to fall off the break from the high side into the hole as it lost all momentum to die perfectly into the cup. Twice he practiced the speed of his hands with what Jaime called a pendulum motion, moving the putter, and then adjusted his stance to the ball and stroked. He knew he would make the putt as the ball left the putter face and began its roll. Juan Jose listened for the magical sound as it slowed and then fell into the cup as foreseen.

"An eagle!" Luis cried out, as if Juan Jose had done something uncanny.

"Congratulations!" Jaime said as he reached for a knuckle bump.

Juan Jose didn't understand why they were making such a fuss over something that was so naturally easy – at least for him. He also didn't know how to respond as Jaime thrust his knuckles of his right fist toward him. He backed away to avoid the blow.

Jaime laughed and said, "This is a celebration of your fine score. You make a knuckle fist like me and we bump them lightly together. I forget how many of my country's customs are different and strange to you."

Juan Jose made the knuckle fist and concluded the bump with Jaime.

Jaime made his eight-footer and Juan Jose breathed a sigh of relief having expected him to miss it. Juan Jose approached him and gestured for the fist bump congratulation. Jaime seemed to brighten momentarily but then dimmed just as quickly when he stated that he had made another double bogey because of the water penalty shot. Juan Jose wondered why Jaime didn't draw more joy from the beautiful day, the clear sky, spectacular greens, singing parrots, lush fairways and the putt he just made. He noticed that Jaime's focus on his score was dimming his day.

The next hole was tightly lined with trees on both sides of the fairway and large bunkers of sand stood guard under the trees from about 210 to 240 yards away. Juan Jose visualized a straight shot going right down the middle, well away from all of the trouble. He realized in his mental preparation that his mind was better equipped for making a good shot if he looked only at the lush green fairway where he wanted his ball to land while forgetting entirely about the trouble to both sides. The ball followed the flight of his visualization and landed about 300 yards down the fairway.

Jaime finally hit a straight drive and his ball carried about 200 yards and rolled to about 215. His next shot was with a three-wood since he was still about 200 yards away. Juan Jose noticed the tenseness in Jaime's arms and his furrowed brow and gritted teeth. Jaime's hands seemed to be clinching the club instead of holding it firm but relaxed. His backswing was very fast and he lunged downward at the ball trying to swing too hard with his arms. He hit the ball with the inside heel of the club and it squirted left bumping along the ground.

"Aiii!" he screamed out. "That was awful! A good way to mess up a good drive."

Juan Jose said sincerely, "I think you were trying too hard to hit the ball far and just tensed up. Relaxed shoulder muscles and arms always helped me swing the sickle in long smooth strokes."

Jaime said, "That is the great dilemma of the golfing experience for struggling amateurs worldwide. You gotta relax to hit the ball properly but by hitting the ball improperly and getting bad results it is impossible to relax. I know I am often going to get an undesirable result and so I am tense and the tenseness brings the undesirable shot about. It is maddening."

"Smile at the golf ball."

"What? I think I misheard you say to smile at the ball."

"Smile at the golf ball when you address it and as you take your next swing."

"What ever in the world for?"

"When you are smiling, it is impossible to grit your teeth. When your teeth are not gritted, your jaw is relaxed. When your jaw is relaxed, your neck muscles are relaxed. When your neck muscles are relaxed, your shoulders are relaxed. And when your shoulders are..."

"Enough already! I get the point and I'll try it."

Jaime stood over the ball with his five-iron and Juan Jose reminded him to smile. Juan Jose noticed the tension disappear from Jaime's body. He made the best swing Juan Jose had seen him make all day and the ball sped through the air toward the green.

"You're a genius!" Jaime praised him.

Juan Jose was embarrassed to be called a genius and so he said nothing and walked on to his ball. He addressed the 115-yard shot with his sand wedge and remembered to try and land beyond the flagstick and to back the ball into the hole. He grinned at the ball and swung. Straight at the flagstick it flew and backed toward the hole missing it by only a few inches.

"Automatic birdie," Jaime said. "You almost backed the ball into the cup for another eagle."

Juan Jose was too busy talking to Luis and learning about his family to reply to Jaime. He was saddened to learn that Luis' older sister had become sick and died just two days ago. She was not taken to the doctor because her husband could not find the use of a burro to make the long walk to carry her to the clinic two hours away from the tiny village where she had lived.

"There are too many early deaths of too many people in our country and for this I am very sad," said Juan Jose.

The day was not as pretty as before this conversation and the golf was suddenly less important and not as much fun as he thought about Luis' sister dying.

Jaime two-putted his 15 feet distance to the hole and Juan Jose tapped in for a birdie.

Still troubled by the death of Luis' sister, he asked Jaime, "Why do so many of my country's children and adults have to die before they get old?"

"They don't have to die, Juan Jose," he said. "That's why our churches send missionaries into your country, so that we can help keep people from dying young and improve things."

"But, your country already has these things that keep people from dying young. Does that mean that God likes your country more than mine?"

"No. God loves your country just as much. 'Blessed are the poor in spirit for theirs is the kingdom of heaven. Blessed are they that mourn: for they shall be comforted.' Learning to trust God in all circumstances is difficult but is an important part of discovering truth," Jaime said.

"I think I understand – that some joy can be found even amid sorrow," Juan Jose confirmed.

He thought about reminding Jaime of this statement on the next hole as Jaime's tee shot flew errantly into the pond on the right side of the fairway. Juan Jose did not have to work as hard as Jaime in finding joy. His drive was straight down the middle about 310 yards.

Jaime dropped a new ball from the point of entry into the lateral water hazard while explaining the penalty rule again to Juan Jose. Juan Jose asked Jaime if he knew why his ball had sliced toward the water. He said he hadn't a clue, so Juan Jose explained.

"You lined your feet up left to avoid the water. However, your shoulders and thighs were pointing down the center of the fairway. When you took your swing, all you could do was to cut across the outside of the ball and make it spin right toward the water. I hope you don't mind my observation."

"Thanks for the help. Perhaps you can check my alignment before I hit next time," Jaime said.

"Just remember that hazards must be faced. With courage, the ball can be made to turn away at just the right moment, leaving both the ball and the obstacle unharmed," Juan Jose said.

"Negotiate around obstacles, leaving both ball and hazard unharmed," Jaime said. "I'll have to remember that."

He took out his three-wood and began to align himself for the green. Juan Jose noticed his alignment was good this time so he said nothing. His backswing was rushed like the people moving through Tegucigalpa. His downswing consequently was off tempo and he hit the ball with his weight toward the rear foot. The ball sailed to the right, missing the green by 50 yards or more.

"Your alignment was very good," Juan Jose said positively.

"Then why did I get the same result?" he said perturbed.

"There are many ways to get to my village. The way over the mountain and through the valley is the most sure because there is a path. The way through the rushing river is faster but oftentimes people drown in the rushing waters and never make it to solid ground. Your swing must be like the long steady path over the mountains. The path is slower than the rushed one but it more often delivers oneself to his destination. *Comprende?*"

"Yes, very perceptive of you to notice my rushed backswing."

The conversation stopped briefly as Juan Jose approached his ball and struck it with his eight-iron to send it toward the backside of the flagstick. The ball backed toward the hole but he could tell it did not go in and had rolled away to the right.

As they approached Jaime's 50-yard half-wedge shot Juan Jose said, "Jaime, I want you to think about taking the club back through a giant tub of molasses."

Jaime's club traveled back in a beautiful, smooth, fluid motion and his weight transferred properly to the right side. His downswing was a nice tempo and he connected solidly with the ball as it sailed 10 yards past the green into the distant side grass bunker.

"I can't believe how far that went with so little effort."

"It is important to learn how to have more with less," Juan Jose said.

As they neared the green Juan Jose saw that his ball was four feet downside of the cup toward the right. He thought about how much closer he could get the ball if he knew in advance about the slopes and characteristics of the greens.

Jaime stood over his ball in the grass bunker and Juan Jose observed his downhill lie. He stood normal over the ball and tried to chip onto the green but his wedge hit the top half of the ball as it rocketed across the green and onto the distant fringe.

Juan Jose thought about the tilt of Jaime's shoulders preceding his shot. His shoulders were kept level and to Juan Jose this looked all wrong. Juan Jose remembered how to stand when swinging the sickle to clear land down a mountainside. He visualized leaning up the mountainside with his legs while tilting his shoulders to match the downward slope of the mountain. This assured a clean sweep of the sickle back down the slope. Juan Jose sensed that tilting one's shoulder to match the slope would work well for downhill and uphill lies in golf as well.

Jaime two-putted from the fringe for an eight and Juan Jose knocked down his four foot putt for a birdie. Luis asked how long he had been playing golf to be so accomplished. When Juan Jose told him it was his first round Luis laughed loudly and called him a great storyteller.

The fifth hole was a par three over a large pond of water. It was playing about 185 yards with a slight breeze behind them. Juan Jose chose his eight-iron but before addressing the ball he asked Luis if he would tell him about the slope of the green and about the break from where the hole was positioned.

"The green slopes right to left towards the front," Luis replied. "You want to be long enough to make it up the first rise but not too long or you'll hit another tier. There are about ten feet in front of the cup and ten feet in back with which to work."

"Then I will try to play the ball long of the hole to the right for a chance to go in," Juan Jose said.

"Have you ever had an ace?" Luis said.

"What's an ace?" Juan Jose said.

"You're teasing me again. *Uno. No mas,*" he said. "A perfect golf shot. A hole-in-one. You know."

"Never have," Juan Jose said with a chuckle – amused that Luis didn't believe this to be his first round of golf.

Juan Jose picked his target to the right of the pin and beyond it. He took extra precaution in aligning his feet, shoulders and thighs. He thought of the warm sun and beautiful scenery surrounding him, then smiled and started his swing back and through as he watched the ball dance majestically high into the air and drop to the target area. The ball backed toward the hole, gathering speed with the slope of the green. They were too far away to see the result but Juan Jose knew he had played the shot well.

Humberto yelled excitedly, "Get in the hole!"

Jaime said, "Fine shot, my friend. Would you like to hit mine?"

Juan Jose was ready to hit his if Jaime had handed him the club but instead Jaime addressed his ball. Juan Jose pictured him making the perfect swing.

"Molasses," he whispered.

However, Jaime swung back rushed, jerked at the top of his backswing and hurried downward. The ball made a loud *crack* and flew at a low height toward the green. Landing hard, the ball skipped past the pin toward the backside of the green.

"Not a solid hit," he said. "But at least I'm on the dance floor about a mile from the cup."

"You forgot about molasses," Juan Jose reminded him.

"It's hard for me to slow my Type-A pace down," Jaime said.

Juan Jose didn't know what he meant by a Type-A, but he figured if Jaime was an A then he must be a Z himself. They walked over a small bridge that led to the green and Juan Jose was busy observing the fish in the water when Luis exclaimed loudly.

"You're in the hole! You aced it! You must be in the hole! I don't see your ball!"

"I finally did something right," Juan Jose said. "I never could have done it without you helping me understand the break of the green, Luis."

Juan Jose retrieved his ball from the bottom of the cup and he received pats on the back and whooping and hollering from all. Juan Jose could not understand all of the commotion and carrying on for having finally done what every golfer is trying to do on every shot to the green.

Humberto tended the pin for Jaime's putt. He putted the ball too hard for the downhill putt and it raced past the cup and settled 10 feet away. Coming back up the hill he putted too soft and the ball came to rest a foot away from the cup. Jaime finished with a three-putt bogey.

Jaime spoke seriously, "Juan Jose, you have a God-given talent for this game. Did you know there are golfers that get paid enormous amounts of money when winning a match? They play golf as their job."

"How can one be paid for something that is not work?" Juan Jose said.

"Golf is their work," he said.

Juan Jose simply shook his head in wonderment that someone would pay money to the winner of a golf game. "And probably a week's worth of wages," he mumbled, since Jaime had said enormous money.

"Tell me more about your sister who died," Juan Jose said solemnly to Luis.

"Her name was Tamara," he said. "She had beautiful eyes and was always laughing, even when she grew sick. At twenty years old she was the oldest of my seven brothers and sisters. We miss her very much."

"My sister María had twins and they both died when they were first born," Juan Jose said. "But now she has a beautiful baby named Angelina. I have seen many of our village children die over the years. Jaime tells me that in our country we have a much higher infant death rate than where he comes from, although, we were able to save some newborn twins because of a missionary doctor the other night."

"It is sad that we lose so many," Luis said somberly.

"Yes, my friend Jaime comes to our village to try to make some of the sadness go away. Their doctors have saved several of the village babies with their medicine and skills," and Juan Jose continued to tell him of Melci's twins being saved by the American doctor and how the twins' names were Luis and Humberto, just like his and the other caddie.

Their conversation carried them to the sixth hole. The little map showed a 427-yard par four with the green protected by three sand bunkers. The hole was straight and long so Juan Jose decided to make the ball turn left slightly or draw as Jaime called it. This shot seemed to go farther than the straight drive. He hit the ball as he had visualized the shot.

Jaime stated out loud that he was going to smile and swing back in molasses. He executed his best drive of the day as he struck the ball solidly and transferred his weight properly. The ball landed within 50 yards of Juan Jose's.

"Best drive I've ever hit!"

They walked to his ball and calculated that he had hit the drive about 260 yards. This left a 167-yard shot to the green and he chose his six-iron. Jaime made a good swing again and the ball landed on the green toward the right side of the hole.

"That felt great," Jaime said. "Two shots in a row. That's all I need to keep me coming back to play some more."

Juan Jose observed that Jaime's enjoyment of the game greatly depended upon how he hit his shots. His mood could change very quickly from sore anger to hopeful joy. Even though Juan Jose had declared to himself, several holes back, to never put his ball into the sand, he now decided to knock his ball into the trap because it would make Jaime feel good to know that his shot to the green was better than his. Also, he wanted the challenge of learning a new shot.

"Misjudged that one," Juan Jose fibbed as his ball flew into the right side bunker.

"That's the first shot you've missed all day," Jaime said. "We were beginning to think we were playing with a deity. Nice to see that you are human too."

Juan Jose inquired about how to play the shot from the sand. Jaime explained explosion shots beginning with the short, high explosion to be used when a ball in the sand is 10 yards or less to the cup. Juan Jose positioned himself for the 10-yard shot to the pin from the sand trap. He picked out a grain of sand two inches behind the ball and swung along his open stance alignment through this target. The ball flew nicely into the air and landed a foot to the right of the flagstick and stopped quickly for an easy two-foot putt.

"Well done," Jaime congratulated him.

Luis entered the trap behind him with the rake he had picked up near the bunker and began to smooth Juan Jose's foot tracks away. Juan Jose said he would be happy to rake his own footprints but Luis said this was his job to do.

Jaime studied his ten-foot birdie putt and made a smooth stroke through the ball. The ball broke slightly left at the cup and settled nicely into the center of the hole.

"A birdie. Yippie!" Jaime exclaimed with joy.

Juan Jose fist-bumped him, tapped in his par and commented on how Jaime had beaten him on that hole. Of course, he had intentionally hit the sand but he felt satisfied at seeing Jaime joyful and in learning a new shot himself.

Number seven was a 541-yard par five with a big dogleg left. The green was protected by water across the front and three large sand traps lay in front of the water shortening the lay up zone.

"A draw shot would serve me well to begin this hole," said Juan Jose as he stepped away from the tee box after remembering that Jaime had the honors as they called it and would be hitting first.

Jaime's alignment was left and he cut across the ball slightly and made it turn the wrong direction at about 200 yards down the fairway. However, it stayed inbounds in the rough. Juan Jose played the draw shot and the ball was struck solidly dead center from the driver – another 300-yard drive that turned into the dogleg.

As they walked to Jaime's ball, Jaime spoke to Juan Jose, "I would like to take you to the United States as my guest and establish your handicap and have you compete to earn the right to play as a professional. Golfers who consistently shoot low rounds earn the right to compete for a spot as a touring professional."

"I'd like to go, but as you know I earn very little money clearing the fields with my sickle," Juan Jose said. "I could never save up enough to go on a trip. I must use my daily earnings for food."

"I'll advance you the money. We'll need to establish a

handicap for you by playing rounds daily when we get to the US. You can pay me back someday from your winnings," Jaime said.

Juan Jose did not understand what Jaime was referring to regarding a handicap and he still couldn't believe that people are paid to do something as enjoyable as golf and that Jaime had mentioned "daily." He wondered who pays them and what service they are providing for the exchange of money. The question lingered in his mind so he asked Jaime.

Jaime explained, "Advertisers put up the money because the people they're trying to reach in their market are the ones watching these golfing events on TV. Billions and billions of dollars are spent by consumers in the golf industry worldwide and on high-end products and services consumed by this demographic."

Juan Jose didn't understand about TV, advertisers, marketing, high-end products or demographics, but instead began to pray for the joy of the day and to give God thanks for sending it his way.

Jaime stood over his ball in the rough and plowed his three-wood through the grass, advancing the ball about 180 yards with a good lie in the fairway. He would be left with a 161 yard shot over the trouble to the green.

They walked to Juan Jose's ball in silence as Juan Jose viewed the lush green fairway and beautiful trees. The warm sun felt good on his face and he once again began to enjoy the day simply for its presence, not thinking about the future or the past. The same thing occurred to him as he stood over his ball and forgot about the drive that had gotten him here and forgot about the planning he had made for the next 231 yards. Now was the time to enjoy the present – to let the swing take over from the past and lead him into the future. The ball pinged off the three-iron and flew toward the distant green.

"Shooting for another eagle are you?" said Jaime.

"Yes, I will try to get it in the hole on the next shot," Juan Jose said.

Juan Jose offered to carry his bag for Luis because he thought Luis was probably getting tired by now.

Luis gave him the strangest look and explained to him, "My job is to carry your bag so that your shoulders do not get tired and so you can keep making all of those great shots. Thank you for your kind offer, though."

Juan Jose was confused again to think that some people get paid to play golf – enormous amounts of money as Jaime had told him and he wondered why Luis, who did all of the work, would still be poor.

Jaime asked Humberto for his five-iron. The trouble in front of the green was influencing his decision to over-club. Juan Jose thought that the six-iron would have been the perfect choice for him. Jaime struck the five-iron solidly knocking the ball into the back bunker.

"I was afraid of the trouble in front so I found the trouble in back," he said.

"Fear causes one to not always see clearly," Juan Jose said.

"And fear causes the worst to happen. That's why they call them hazards on the golf course."

"If you can avoid the fear, you can avoid most of the hazards," Juan Jose said.

"Ah, but it is the same dilemma that faces the golfer who does not make a good swing consistently and so therefore does not relax. To have no fear requires total confidence in one's ability to clear the hazard."

Juan Jose could see that golf made Jaime think too much and that only a succession of the purest of shots could deliver him from his rut or dilemma as he called it.

Like a waterfall of white that breaks the greenness of a mountainside, Juan Jose found great pleasure in seeing the white dot sitting on the green blanket of beautiful bent grass. His ball lay neatly on the green about 30 feet from the cup. Jaime's ball from the back bunker was about 20 yards from the cup so he began explaining the medium bunker shot to Juan Jose. Juan Jose made a mental note of the adjustments required for a medium explosion shot and watched as Jaime executed nicely. The ball came out of the bunker low and landed about five yards from the cup and then ran another 10 feet.

"I wanted a five foot or less uphill putt," said Jaime. "Every once in a while things work out the way I've planned."

Juan Jose realized that even Jaime's positive comments contained a tinge of negativism as he mused, this dueling force of good thoughts and bad ones surely distract from the positive focus Jaime needs to play this game well.

Looking over his 30-foot putt, Juan Jose noticed a three-foot break and a fast downhill to the hole. He chose his target about 20 feet away and figured the ball would run the rest of the way down to the hole. Juan Jose thought of the ball dropping into the cup and visualized both the sight and sound of the completed putt as he stroked the ball confidently. He knew it was in the hole the minute his eyes left the putter that had struck the ball squarely. Now, he waited for the putt to catch up to his intuition and drop neatly into the cup.

"Another eagle!" Luis exclaimed excitedly.

"*Magnífico!*" chimed in Humberto.

Everyone fist bumped Juan Jose in celebration.

Jaime said, "You will be paid richly someday for your great skill."

Juan Jose thought to himself how he had already been paid richly by his opportunity to play the game today. Being outside on such a beautiful day at this golf course paradise, while enjoying the fine walk across the course with his friend Jaime and his new friends Luis and Humberto, was rich enough payment for him.

The next hole awaiting them was a 212-yard par three which was all carry over a lake. The water extended around the entire right side. The left front contained a sand bunker and both the left side and back side were surrounded by trees after a brief planting of about 10 yards of rough. Juan Jose chose his six-iron and decided to carry the ball over the water back into the green with a draw so that the ball would run toward the pin nestled on the back left side of the green. Once again he relaxed completely and forgot about the water by thinking only about the green and how his ball would land. The ball performed as envisioned and ran toward the pin stopping about three feet from the cup.

Jaime's first shot kerplunked into the water about 10 yards to the right of the green. He overcompensated and hooked the next one into the trees on the left side of the green as they heard a loud *"Kuuwackkk!"* The ball ricocheted off the tree back toward the green and rolled to within 20 feet of the cup.

"That's a churchgoer's shot," Jaime said with a smile. "Cause only God could have made that ugly shot end up on the green."

Juan Jose chuckled to himself at Jaime's joke and was glad that Jaime could occasionally look at his bad golf shots with humor instead of frustration. Jaime actually made his 20 foot putt. Juan Jose wondered if Jaime's humorous attitude toward the bad tee shot and more relaxed attitude might be related to how well he had putted the ball.

"Routine bogey," he said.

Juan Jose made his birdie putt and they headed to the ninth hole. Luis informed Juan Jose that he would shatter the course record for the front nine even if he bogeyed or double-bogeyed the hole. Juan Jose found it hard to comprehend that his score would be the best on the course since he had only one perfect shot – the ace on number five.

The ninth hole was a 425 yard par four that played to an elevated green guarded by water on the right and five bunkers. He hit a big tee shot straight down the middle with a slight draw. Jaime hit a good straight shot although his was 70 or more yards short of Juan Jose's. Jaime played his 200 yards remaining with his three-wood and landed in a front side bunker short of the green. Juan Jose played his 100 yard shot with an intuitive three-quarters swing of his sand wedge and knew that he was close enough to birdie the hole. Jaime explained the long explosion shot since Juan Jose had already been instructed in both the short and medium shots and Jaime was about to play a long one.

"You play the shot with your normal grip," he said. "On this shot you want the clubhead to turn over at impact and through the ball. Position the ball just forward of the center of your stance. Since I am more than 20 yards to the pin, I will play this shot with my pitching wedge instead of my sand wedge."

"I think I understand the subtle differences between the long, middle and short sand explosion shots," Juan Jose said. "Do you still hit the sand two inches behind the ball on the long one?"

"Same thing on all of them," Jaime said.

Jaime made another fine sand shot that rolled to within four feet of the cup as he explained, "I should be in the sand more often."

They both made their putts and Jaime congratulated Juan Jose on the most outstanding half-round of golf that he had ever witnessed. Juan Jose noticed that Jaime went into the clubhouse at the turn with the scorecard in hand. The golf pro came out to speak to Juan Jose. He was a handsome Spaniard named Roberto Ramón with jet black hair and neatly trimmed mustache. He wore fine golfing attire with a colorful white knit shirt with burgundy stripes and the club logo that read *Paraíso Trópico* and underneath *Tegucigalpa Green Tee Club*. His bronze face had a square jaw and large brown eyes that pierced through Juan Jose as he spoke.

"Did you really shoot this score?"

"Well, yes it is correct," Juan Jose replied sincerely. He did not understand the significance of the feat he had accomplished.

Luis chimed in, "He's the greatest golfer I've ever seen. I think that he could beat even you. His score is correct. The strokes were easy to count – they were so few."

"No one can shoot a 25 front nine on this course," he said as his eyes narrowed.

Juan Jose was insulted that their honesty was being questioned over a fun game that he had just learned. Did Roberto Ramón's question mean that some golfers actually cheat while playing a round? Juan Jose thought about the value of honor and how much more you can gain by being truthful. Why would anyone give away their peace-of-mind over a dishonest golf score? The game must indeed have some strange power over people if it can make them cheat.

Jaime said, "Twenty-five is correct and attested by all of us. Perhaps you would like to join us on the back nine and witness firsthand the purest swing in golf?"

"Yes, I would be honored to play alongside such a great golfer as Juan Jose," he said to soothe the implication that Juan Jose had cheated.

Roberto arranged for his caddie Eduardo to join them. They strode toward the tenth hole and Juan Jose let Roberto walk in the lead since he seemed to be annoyed if anyone got in front of him.

The tenth hole was a 344 yard par four. The elevated tee box looked down a magnificent fairway lined with trees on the right side while the left side held a creek that flowed into a large pond about 230 yards down the fairway. The pond stood in front of a towering green about 20 yards higher than the fairway and water. Three sand traps lay threatening at the front side of the green. From the lay up area, the second shot would be all carry to the elevated green. A shot too long would roll off the backside into the trees.

Jaime tossed a tee into the air and it pointed to Roberto. "You have the honors," Jaime said to Roberto.

Again he tossed the tee and it pointed to Juan Jose.

"You will be next, my friend," Jaime said. "And I will be last as usual. This was probably my only opportunity to go first," he added.

Once again, Juan Jose noticed Jaime's negative statement about himself and he wondered where the hope that Jaime talked about in their village had vanished – the confidence that comes from living and doing the right things.

Roberto stepped assuredly to his ball and took his stance. Juan Jose noticed he had selected a four-iron. He had a slow backswing and was very balanced and in control. Juan Jose could tell that his shot was going to be a good one even before he hit the ball. The ball sailed to about 200 yards and bounced another 10 down the fairway to a perfect position.

"Muy bien," Juan Jose commented as he moved to the tee box.

He decided that he wanted to equal Roberto's shot and he calculated that his six-iron would land him in the same spot 210 yards down the fairway.

"Is there any penalty if I hit your ball?" Juan Jose said, since he wanted to be exactly where Roberto's ball was in the fairway.

"I'll give you 2,000 *lempira* (about $90 U.S.) if you hit my ball," he challenged.

Juan Jose couldn't believe what he had just heard. Two-thousand *lempira* would take him weeks to earn in the fields with his sickle. He took extra care to align himself precisely and then swung with joy. The ball landed at the 200 yard area and bounced toward Roberto's ball. They could see the two white orbs nestled together from the elevated tee box. He hoped that his ball was touching Roberto's but he could not be certain until they walked closer.

Roberto gasped, "Ohhhhh! Surely you didn't! I know they won't be touching. The odds aren't in your favor. That'd be like making a hole-in-one."

"Yes, I only made one ace on the front nine," Juan Jose said humbly.

"*No es possible*," Roberto said. "It just can't be."

Jaime whacked his ball with his three-wood and the ball sailed toward the trees on the right about 200 yards. Juan Jose hoped that the ball would stay out of the trees so that Jaime would have a clear shot to the green. He noticed that Jaime's push to the right seemed to result from leaving his weight on his right side and not carrying through correctly, so he commented.

"When facing a huge clump of grain with my sickle, I must swing back through with all my power. My weight is thrown toward the target with the rotation."

"You must be referring to weight transfer back to the left, and yes, I'm aware of my shortcomings."

"Preparation is the key. You don't want to rush into things halfway and forget to finish – especially when cutting thick grain, but I suppose the same can be said of striking the golf ball."

"I see," Jaime said as they arrived at his ball.

Fortunately, Jaime's ball was not in the trees and he could shoot for the green. He chose his seven-iron and Juan Jose noticed his backswing was much slower and his weight transferred better to his right and better rotation to his left. He finished high, admiring his well struck shot. He was on the green, although with a long downhill putt remaining from the back with a treacherous double break.

Roberto was the first to arrive at their balls and Juan Jose noticed him pulling money from his pocket. As Juan Jose approached him, Roberto handed him the 2,000 *lempira*.

"You're the luckiest person I ever met!"

As Juan Jose took the money a strange sensation came over him as he thought about how easily he had just made several weeks' of wages and wondered what is the meaning of this?

The money seemed to burn in his hand. He knew that his next shot would be difficult to make with these strange sensations and thoughts within him. He turned to Luis and handed him the two 1,000 *lempira* bills.

"Please accept this as my gratitude for you carrying my golf bag today and assisting me," Juan Jose said. "I would like the money to be used to pay for the burial of your oldest sister."

Luis was overwhelmed with emotion and his eyes became watery as he said, *"Muchas gracias, señor. Muchas gracias."*

Roberto asked Juan Jose to hit next since their balls were exactly even and he placed a marker a putter-head's length away as if moving a ball marker on the putting green. Juan Jose chose his wedge for the 130 yard shot and landed several feet beyond the pin. The ball backed up just missing the hole. The two foot uphill putt would be very simple to make for a birdie, but Juan Jose was disappointed that he had missed the eagle. Roberto replaced his ball in the fairway and landed 10 feet to the right of the pin.

Roberto said, "I am very impressed with your golf swing. Where did you learn to play the game and how long have you been playing?"

"I learned from Jaime. This is my first game."

Roberto grinned and said, "Sure, I believe you. I think I've been had. Are you related to a professional golfer?"

"Don't know any professional golfers."

"Right," is all that Roberto said.

Once again, Juan Jose knew that Roberto questioned his honesty in these simple answers and Juan Jose was confused, thinking, why would anyone lie about a golf game?

Jaime three-putted for a bogey. Roberto two-putted for a par and Juan Jose knocked in his easy birdie. He began to study the scorecard picture of the eleventh hole that showed four hundred yards with a river halfway up the left side and the green nestled on the far left as well. A large bunker lay next to the water off the fairway from about 200 to 250 yards. This sand would not come into play for a 300-yard drive. Juan Jose decided he would simply carry the sand with a straight shot over both water and sand to the middle of the fairway.

As he began to align himself over the ball Roberto said, "Swing fast and hard if you're going to go over that water and sand down the left side."

Not taken in by his comment, Juan Jose said, "I always swing the same, neither too fast nor too hard. Those who are too fast don't enjoy the journey and hardly get to where they're going."

The ball rocketed low off the tee lifting like a soccer ball kicked from midfield. It soared past the sand and water and dropped down to begin a long roll to the center of the fairway.

Roberto's shot was 250 yards to the right-center of the fairway away from the sand and Juan Jose's drive was 320 yards and well beyond the hazard. Jaime's drive was 230 yards in the middle of the fairway.

Roberto said, "You really crushed that one, Juan Jose. Are you always that long off the tees?"

Juan Jose said, "I hit that one straight because of the surroundings but I can make it go further moving the ball from right to left."

Roberto said, "Different people reach their destination

by different means and that is what keeps the game from being dull."

Jaime asked Roberto if he knew about spiritual destination and where the final green would be found. Roberto stared back dumbfounded but Juan Jose understood the meaning to his question.

Juan Jose took in a deep breath of the fresh countryside air and stooped to pick up a leaf in the fairway to examine on this fine walk toward Jaime's ball. The webbing beneath the leaf, which he looked at closely, resembled an entire tree with smaller branches growing from the main trunk. He wondered at the way the leaf was distinctive from both sides of ribs but was held together as a perfect unit by its very different members. He thought of the missionaries like Jaime, from another country, who are different but have bonded together with his villagers to help them.

Jaime pulled out his five-wood for the 170 yards remaining. The water in front of the green shone brightly reflecting the sun. Single sand bunkers stood lookout to both sides forming a narrow entrance to the green. Jaime hit his shot about 180 yards and it rolled through the green and off the back.

"Safe," he said.

Juan Jose thought to himself. If you are only trying to be safe on the golf course, then how can you ever reach your highest potential? To succeed requires some risk.

Roberto selected an eight-iron from 150 yards out. He made a fine shot toward the flagstick but the ball held in the breeze before descending and came up 10 yards short.

Juan Jose's distance called for an 80 yard shot and he gripped down slightly on his lob wedge to execute the same three-quarters swing he had used on his last 100 yard shot with the sand wedge. As the ball flew toward the pin he could see it was straight on target. The ball hit the flagstick in the air and ricocheted off toward the right.

"Even perfection can sometimes go awry on the golf course," he said as he contemplated the fate of that shot and wondered what meaning was to be found in a random circumstance that changed his direction. He decided that his response to the ill-fated stroke was to overcome the adversity and put his next shot into the hole even though the ball had ricocheted all the way into the rough just past the fringe of the green.

Jaime chipped from the back of the green. Juan Jose observed closely and asked him to explain how to execute this shot.

"Different golfers use different methods," he said. "I like to use the lowest lofted club possible to get the ball onto the surface of the green and then let the roll carry the ball toward the hole. If you are very close to the hole this may mean using your sand wedge. I de-loft the club by playing the ball off my back foot with my feet close together in an open stance. I put most of my weight on my left side and grip down on the club to execute a putting stroke and get the ball into the air to my landing spot just a few feet onto the green. The toe of the club is pointed down and the heel is up."

Jaime's seven-iron chip ran toward the cup and stopped only a foot short. Juan Jose liked the accurateness of his method and chose his regular pitching wedge to chip the ball one-third of the way onto the green and figured the ball would roll the other two-thirds. He picked a mark on the green to land the ball after accounting for the break and the ball's final destination. He thought of the sound of the ball dropping into the hole and visualized the ball landing on the exact spot chosen. The ball rolled perfectly to the hole and struck the pin with a crisp *chink* sound.

Roberto said, "Nice chip. Now the pressure's on me."

Juan Jose wondered why Roberto was pressured since this seemed to be a game to be enjoyed. The design of the course through nature was the perfect place to relax, and he didn't care to have any self-inflicted pressure.

Roberto studied his break from both ends of the putt and spent extra long in his pre-shot routine. Finally, he stroked the 25 footer and it traveled perfectly to the hole.

"That's better," he said. "Can't believe I gave you a stroke by two-putting that last hole."

Suddenly, Juan Jose became aware that Roberto was playing against him to beat his score and not playing for the pure enjoyment of the game. *How could I have so mistaken the point of this game?*

Juan Jose determined that he would continue to play within himself, accountable for his own outcome and not pay much attention to Roberto's. When the game is over will be the proper time for determining a winner. The result would take care of itself. The steps along the way were what mattered to Juan Jose – the blue sky, green trees, pretty greens, still waters, company of his friends and best of all – to watch the white ball fly unbelievably high and far through the air like a speeding bird.

The 521-yard 12th hole had a beautiful tee box with trees lining both sides for the first 100 yards. The tee box was elevated and Juan Jose looked down a lush green valley of fairway leading the way to the par five hole. He still had the honors and he crushed his driver extra-long with the slope of the land to aid him and the slight draw that he played on the ball.

"That's huge!" Roberto said. "You're a hard act to follow."

Juan Jose said, "If you wish to go before me on the next hole, I don't mind."

Roberto looked at him strangely and said, "So you don't think I have a chance to win this hole, do you?"

"Yes, chance is a part of the game. On the last hole it was by chance that my ball struck the pin and left me a difficult shot. If you execute better than I, then you will win the hole. I would never leave it to chance."

Juan Jose could tell that he had aggravated Roberto when all he was trying to do was to be polite and let him go first even if he did not win the honors. There was something about his demeanor that offended Juan Jose, like Roberto was always jabbing at him with a sharp knife intended to pierce his calm emotion. The point had landed squarely back upon Roberto even without Juan Jose trying and he could see from the tension in Roberto's face that this would not be one of his better drives. His backswing was a little rushed and Juan Jose thought he tried to swing too hard as the ball drew way too far left and banged into the trees on the left side. Juan Jose saw his ball bound back into the fairway. Roberto let out a string of offensive language that involved *Nuestro Señor*. Why would one curse God for one's own stupid golf shot? Juan Jose questioned to himself.

"You're in the fairway, and still have a chance," Juan Jose said to calm him down.

"You saw my ball come back into the fairway?" he said. "Praise the Lord!"

Juan Jose thought to himself. As if the Lord cares if your golf ball goes into the fairway or the trees. Our Creator has better things to do than to follow the little white ball of someone who is cursing and praising Him in the same breaths.

Jaime hit a short drive safely with his three-wood which Juan Jose thought was a wise decision. Jaime completely ignored Roberto's offensive cursing and Juan Jose admired him for his calm.

Juan Jose separated himself from Roberto on the stroll down the fairway. Jaime chose to walk at Juan Jose's slow pace as well, instead of with Roberto.

Jaime whispered to Juan Jose, "I'm sorry that I asked him to play with us. Please forgive me."

"You've done nothing wrong. I'll forgive Roberto instead."

"You're a good man, Juan Jose."

Jaime knocked the three-wood shot another 210 yards down the fairway. Juan Jose appreciated the way Jaime was beginning to play within himself and adjust to the things he told Jaime were wrong with his swing.

Roberto's ball was laying perfectly in the fairway at 290 yards from the green. He chose to lay up with his three-wood and declared that he would birdie the hole thanks to the lucky tree that put his ball back into the fairway.

Juan Jose chose his seven-iron for the remaining 200 downhill yards to the green. Just before he aligned himself, Roberto interrupted, "One hundred *lemps* if you hit the green, but you pay me two hundred if you don't."

Juan Jose knew that Roberto was trying to confuse him by distracting him for an advantage as well as put him under pressure, so once again he ignored him. Juan Jose asked Luis to describe the slope of the green. Since the green broke left to right and the pin was at the back Juan Jose decided to focus to the left of the flagstick at the back fringe. With good backspin and the downhill slope he figured he could get reasonably close to the pin and perhaps even put the ball in the hole. Juan Jose stood over the ball and let his swing happen. The ball soared toward the green landing neatly at the fringe as envisioned and backed toward the hole. He knew that it didn't go in, but he would be putting for an easy eagle.

Roberto reached into his pocket and handed him a 100 *lempira* bill.

Juan Jose refused to take it saying, "I would value your friendship more than your money. I never accepted your bet so the money is still yours."

Roberto seemed perturbed, stating, "One hundred *lemps* is really nothing. Take it. You earned it."

How could this man declare that one hundred *lempira* is really nothing? Hours of picking coffee beans or cutting in the field cannot be called nothing. Juan Jose had heard stories about rich men but he had never met one until today. At the time, he did not realize that Jaime and all of the American missionaries were also rich even though they acted so humbly while visiting his Honduran village. Juan Jose reached out and took the money to appease Roberto and while no one was looking he handed it to Jaime's caddie Humberto.

Juan Jose whispered, "Thank you for carrying my friend's bag."

"Muchas gracias, señor," Humberto said.

Roberto was left with a short pitch to the green and he executed a decent shot to within seven feet of the pin. This shot pleased him but he remarked, "I better not lose this hole with a birdie."

Jaime also pitched to the green but was off target and left his ball 25 feet downhill to the right of the hole. He whispered to Juan Jose, "Drain your putt, *mi amigo.*"

Jaime two putted for par, Roberto made his birdie and Juan Jose stood over his four-foot eagle putt. He had learned the rhythm of putting and that the pre-shot routine of practicing the correct stroke speed was necessary to bring on the proper focus. He stroked the ball and awaited the pleasant sound of the ball dropping into the cup.

"Bien, muy bien!" Jaime exclaimed. "Another eagle!"

As Juan Jose reached into the cup for his ball he noticed that Roberto turned away with a disgusted look on his face. Juan Jose was confused about how his low score seemed to be affecting Roberto. Juan Jose's goal was not to beat him, but to achieve perfection for himself. How could this be the wrong thing to do? He decided to pursue his goal and hoped that Roberto would learn to enjoy his own game, seeking peace through achievement from within.

Juan Jose was amazed to find a water cooler on the course, as if the golf club had known that he would be thirsty right now. His dry mouth yearned for the cool liquid but he stopped to draw water for the rest of the group first. Roberto reached out for the cup of water that Juan Jose was handing to his caddie. He grabbed the cup and guzzled the water, then quickly asked him to refill his cup again before the others were served.

"Would you like some more?" Juan Jose said.

"Uno mas," he demanded.

"My pleasure," Juan Jose said as he handed him his third drink. Juan Jose's own parched mouth longed for a sip but he continued filling cups for the others. Finally, he drank his own cup and thought of how much better the water tasted because of his delayed reward and kindness shown to the others.

"You have a beautiful golf course," Juan Jose said to Roberto.

"It's O.K. I have played much better courses around the world. What is the finest course in the world that you have played?"

"This is the only course I've played and it is the most beautiful place on earth," Juan Jose said.

Roberto shook his head in disgust and turned away from him. Juan Jose looked at Luis and shrugged his shoulders to silently ask why Roberto was angry with him. Luis noticed Juan Jose's hurt look and responded with a quick wink and a smile.

The 417-yard par four 13th hole awaited them. From the tee box the green was hidden from view because of an uphill tee shot and a large tree standing in the target line down the left hand side of the fairway. A three-wood's extra loft, instead of the driver, was necessary in order to clear the tree for good shot positioning in the fairway.

Juan Jose concentrated on the blade of grass two inches

in front of his ball in alignment with the tree and then as he took his swing he watched the ball strike a designated dimple he had chosen as the ball ascended directly down the target line. The shot cleared the tree perfectly. Next, Roberto tried to draw the ball around the tree with his driver but the shot bent too fast and struck the top limb in the tree and ricocheted to the right. Once again the profanities flew angrily from his mouth. Meanwhile, Jaime calmly took his three-wood and knocked his golf ball over the tree.

"I was determined to outdrive you, and it cost me all my distance," Roberto grumbled to Juan Jose.

"You clearly would have outdriven me had it not been for that tree limb," Juan Jose said. "Sometimes power does not get us around obstacles but instead causes the obstacles to become more in the way," he added.

Once more Juan Jose had unintentionally perturbed Roberto. The scowl on Roberto's face and his quickening of pace told Juan Jose that Roberto was angered by his comments.

Roberto's ball lay only 100 yards from the tee box with a clean lie that enabled him to choose the club he should have teed off with – his three-wood. The shot was played well but still came up 85 yards short of the green.

Jaime swung his three-wood again and hit a beautiful shot landing in front of the green. Juan Jose noticed that his tempo gave him a buttery smooth backswing and nice follow-through on the downswing.

"What were you thinking as you stood over the ball?" Juan Jose said.

"Nothing."

"*Perfecto*," Juan Jose said.

Juan Jose paced off the distance from the 150-yard marker and noted his ball was 168 yards from the green. Luis instructed him as to the slope of the green and he picked his nine-iron to travel the uphill distance remaining.

Juan Jose chose a spot to the right of the pin and worked backwards to the blade of grass several inches in front of his ball and then chose the appropriate dimple behind the ball to strike. Back and forth – *Swoosh!* The ball launched high into the air and traveled to his envisioned spot on the green. The group lost sight of the ball because of the uphill green but Juan Jose knew it would be close to the hole.

Roberto pitched to the green as did Jaime. All three balls were within ten feet of the pin with Juan Jose's only two feet away, Roberto's at five feet and Jaime's at ten. Juan Jose was learning how difficult total perfection is to achieve in this game called golf. He fully expected his ball to be in the hole but he had missed by two feet. However, he found deep satisfaction in each of his shots for there was joy in the swinging – even when the shot missed the hole. Par, par and Juan Jose's birdie were recorded on the scorecard as the putts rattled into the cup one by one.

Juan Jose spoke to Jaime, "I thank you so much for this day and for bringing me to this beautiful place to learn this game."

Jaime said, "You're not learning, for you have mastered the game. No one in the world is capable of what you are doing."

"Isn't that true of everyone?" Juan Jose said. "We all have been given gifts."

"Yes, but I'm afraid we sometimes forget to take the wrapping off," Jaime said. "Or the package is lost."

"Well, I'm glad you helped me uncover golf today," Juan Jose said.

The next hole was a 188-yard par three. Juan Jose surveyed the layout from the tee box noticing that a creek ran down the right side and a pond of water protected the left side and the back of the green. Tall sand traps lay in front on both sides as well as the back left side just before the pond. The pin was positioned at the back left hand side.

Juan Jose decided that his eight-iron would be the right club by playing a slight draw with extra carry aided by the breeze at their backs. He remembered his ace from the front nine and thought about how satisfying another perfect shot would be. Roberto had evidently learned his lesson on making silly bets and was uncharacteristically quiet now before Juan Jose's shots. Juan Jose swung toward the pin and watched the ball shoot high into the air and drop toward the flag. The ball struck the flag which wrapped around it for an instant and then dropped down about a foot from the hole.

"Great shot!" Jaime exclaimed. "Almost an ace."

Roberto shook his head bewildered saying, "I think I'm in the presence of someone *muy especiál.*"

Juan Jose was embarrassed that Roberto's comment may have been directed at him. He would never think of himself as more special than someone else.

Roberto hit his shot to the right without enough draw to bring it back toward the pin and was left with 20 feet or more to the hole. Jaime's shot just cleared the front bunker and came up well short of the green.

Roberto questioned Juan Jose more on the walk to the green asking, "Really, where did you learn to play golf? Your swing is pure and true."

Juan Jose replied honestly, "The benefit of a lifetime of hard work."

"We learn by repetition," Roberto said.

"Yes, when I was a young boy following my father into the mountains he would tell me, 'If you want to reach the top, keep your eyes looking toward the peak, but keep walking.' The higher levels are the most difficult to climb, but much more rewarding when reached."

Juan Jose's simple statement ended their conversation but he could tell that Roberto was trying to reason through something he had said as they approached the green.

Jaime and Roberto made pars and Juan Jose sunk another

birdie putt. Roberto frowned as he left the green.

On the way to the 15th hole, Jaime challenged Juan Jose, "If you were a rich man in what ways would you be changed?"

"I would not desire to be changed at all."

"But would you not be changed by the changes taking place around you?"

"When it is cold, water becomes ice. When it is hot, water becomes steam. But water remains water and my being remains me, whether rich or poor."

"Things will change for you when we pursue your golf talent and you are rewarded financially."

"There is only one reason I would desire to make much money. Do you know why?"

Thinking it was a trick question, Jaime asked, "No, why?"

"Because I could do nice things for other people."

"Your wisdom impresses me greatly," Jaime said.

"All wisdom comes from God," Juan Jose said.

The 15th hole was a 410-yard par four. The tee shot demanded accuracy with a long bunker along the right and water protecting the left side. An elevated green sloped drastically left toward the water and deep sand traps with blind shots to the green lined the front. Juan Jose chose a landing area just to the left of the right side bunker so that he could get as close to the hole as possible with his drive. He prepared himself for the drive taking caution to stay tension free and to feel the clubhead of his driver as it accelerated downward through the swing as his left hip cleared and his eyes riveted on the ball as his shoulder passed under his chin. After 14 holes of play he could feel his muscles tightening a bit so he had to pay extra attention to relaxing them for the swing.

"Great drive," Jaime complimented him.

"Thanks," he said humbly.

"How do you stay so consistent?" Roberto said.

"I have swung the sickle all my life and the rhythm is the same," Juan Jose again tried to explain.

Roberto shrugged as if not understanding and turned away as he placed his tee into the earth and began his pre-shot routine. The ball flew far, his best drive of the day.

"I'm staying with you on this one. I must rise to the level of my competition," he said.

Since Roberto's drive was farther and Juan Jose would be hitting first, he knew that if he put his ball into the hole he would help Roberto "rise to the level" as he had said.

Jaime's tee shot landed 220 yards down the fairway with a slight draw and came to rest on the left side just short of the water.

"Whew! That was close to disaster," Jaime said.

"Jaime, why does Roberto want to beat me so badly?" Juan Jose whispered as they walked down the fairway.

"He is a competitor. Someday, you too must play competitively."

"But can't I be kind to others and competitive at the same time?"

"In America, those that can do both are called 'good sports'."

"Then I wish to be a 'good sport'."

"You already are. Don't change a thing and you'll be a great winner, both professionally and personally."

Jaime selected his five-wood since he had more confidence in contacting the ball with that club than with his lower irons. Once again, his ball had a slight draw which was a huge improvement over his earlier shots during the round. His ball flew slightly left of the green and started downhill toward the water.

"Stop! Stop! Whoa ball! Whoa!" he shouted as the ball rolled toward the water. They couldn't see from their position whether or not the ball stopped short of the water.

Juan Jose was amused at the idea of talking to a golf ball as if it had ears and could obey.

For the first time Roberto had outdistanced Juan Jose because Juan Jose had chosen to hit the ball straight whereas Roberto had played a draw. Juan Jose only had a 130 yard shot to the hole so he chose his wedge to make certain the ball reached the elevated green and avoided the front sand traps. Luis reminded him about the steep left-to-right slope so he closed his stance slightly and strengthened his grip to contact the ball to the inside of center and to move it from right to left to land above the pin and take the slope of the green back toward the hole. The ball followed his plan precisely and he knew that it had a chance to go into the hole.

Roberto made a fine shot to the green as well. When they arrived they spotted Jaime's ball just a few feet short of the water. Roberto was three feet from the cup and Juan Jose's had rolled past the cup to within five feet. Juan Jose wondered by how many inches it had missed the cup on its way by the hole and again he pondered the difficulty of being perfect in this game called golf.

Jaime pitched back up to the green about 10 feet from the cup. He two-putted from there for a bogey while both Roberto and Juan Jose sank their birdie putts. His caddie, Luis, told him that with three holes to go he would break the course record, even if he only made par on each of them. Juan Jose birdied the 16th and 18th and shot eagle on the par five 17th hole. Both Roberto and Jaime had pars on the 16th and 18th but Roberto birdied the 17th hole while Jaime bogeyed it.

"Congratulations! You not only set the course record but that should be a world record as well! But, who are you? Really? You must be a professional. Why haven't I heard about you before today?" Roberto said, his eyes bearing down on Juan Jose as if trying to look into his soul.

"A 51! Wow! Outstanding! *Perfecto!*" Jaime exclaimed. "We must get you on the Professional Golf Circuit."

The caddies patted him on the back and requested that he write his name on their scorecards. Roberto continued shaking his head and inquiring who taught Juan Jose to play so well.

"Nuestro Señor," Juan Jose said. "I credit Him with my talent."

"Your father must be a master," Roberto said.

"Sí, He is The Master of us all. He teaches us things that help us find inner peace," Juan Jose said.

"Whatever it is you have, I want it," Roberto demanded.

"Perhaps Jaime can teach you as he has taught me."

Roberto glared at Jaime and said, "I don't think you can teach me anything. I've seen you play."

"Oh no, I'm a pastor and a missionary. I can teach you spiritual truth," said Jaime.

"I don't want religion, I want to shoot 50 and beat Juan Jose," Roberto said in a bitter voice, then turned and walked away.

"Roberto doesn't understand that hope, peace and joy only come from The Source who is greater than oneself," Juan Jose said as he looked at Jaime.

Before heading back to the village, Jaime and Juan Jose made arrangements in Tegucigalpa for Juan Jose's travel visa so that he could visit the United States. Juan Jose felt guilty when he saw Jaime pay for everything, but Jaime assured him that he would be able to pay him back from the earnings from golf when Juan Jose became famous. Jaime promised to return to the village soon after he worked out a schedule of golf competition to earn Juan Jose the right to compete on the Professional Golf Circuit. He left him his set of clubs and told him to continue hitting balls so "the feel" as he described it, wouldn't go away.

Juan Jose was determined to pay for as much of the

trip as possible so every day he walked many miles to avoid the land supervised by Tim Bigelow and hired on with another land owner to clear the distant fields with his sickle and continued to swing to and fro in the hot sun. He still found joy in the swinging although he often thought about the beautiful land on the golf course and the flight of the little white ball. In the evenings he would pick out imaginary flagsticks from the surrounding trees and would make the ball strike the trunks precisely. The village children gathered around him daily and found the balls that he hit and shagged them for him. They were overjoyed to watch the white ball sail into the air and would scream with delight as he prepared to hit the ball. Little did Juan Jose know that their loud and frequent laughter would prepare him for the click of a camera shutter or a cough from someone in the crowd in his future.

Angelina stood close by Juan Jose as an older girl asked if she could try the club. Juan Jose carefully instructed her how to hold the shaft in her small hands. She swung but missed the ball entirely as they all bent over in laughter. Juan Jose reached out for her left hand and the right hand of Angelina and asked the rest of the children to join in. Each child took the hands of two others and around and around in a circle they danced singing a Mexican folk song that had made its way to Honduras – *De Colores!*

4.

Blessed are those who hunger and thirst after righteousness, for they shall be filled.

Many rains came to Juan Jose's village and 60 days passed until one evening as he hit his seven-iron high into the sky and followed the flight downward he saw the red Toyota truck and heard it rumbling into the village. Jaime had returned! All of the children surrounded the truck and as Jaime emerged they hugged his legs while waiting for his fond pat on the head or a hug. Juan Jose noticed that Jaime was clutching a paper with one hand. Juan Jose ran toward the lively reunion.

Jaime warmly embraced Juan Jose and exclaimed, "This newspaper is from Austin, Texas and contains a photo of the scorecard of the lowest round ever recorded!" Jaime translated the article for all as he read:

Local missionary attests the world's lowest recorded round of golf declaring the 51 score as miraculous!

Pastor James Bowles recently traveled to the Agalta Valley where he participated in his twenty-fifth mission trip providing medical, construction and education teams. He innocently placed a golf club into the hands of a Honduran field laborer and discovered the man named Juan Jose Delgado could make the ball fly accurate and true.

Pastor Bowles exclaimed, "The first swing Juan Jose ever made was a thing of great beauty – rhythmic and pure. I knew I was in the presence of a God-given talent that was unlike any other. Juan Jose never missed striking the ball solidly as I handed him different clubs and I knew I must take him to play a round."

They traveled to the Honduran capitol city, Tegucigalpa where Juan Jose recorded the unbelievable score of 51 at the Tegucigalpa Green Tee Club. Pastor Bowles has secured a visa to allow Juan Jose to come to the United States to compete professionally as soon as he qualifies. The Rolling Hills Golf Club of Austin is hosting a first stage Qualifying School consisting of four rounds that will determine the best 10% of the golfers to get to stage two.

Again, Juan Jose rode with Jaime in the horrible traffic, watching the flood of people hurrying along as they drove to the airport through the busy streets of Tegucigalpa. Jaime talked about the golf matches he had arranged and explained that Juan Jose must first qualify at the local level.

"We are going to Austin, Texas so you can play in a local qualifying tournament. To reach the next level, you must finish in the top 10% and do the same in the next tournament," Jaime explained.

"Will 51 shots be good enough to win?"

"Juan Jose, if you shoot another 51 you are going to be the best golfer in the world and yes, you will win."

"How much money does it cost to play?"

"Don't worry about the money. That's what I am here for. You and I are business partners. I have a contract being written by an attorney."

"What does the contract say? Why do we need one?"

"It's just a good thing to put our agreement in writing.

That way if a question ever arises, we can work things out by looking at what is written."

"I am not worried about needing to work things out. Whatever you say will be fine."

"Basically, you will own 49% of our business and I will own 51% and we will give 10% of all our winnings to charity, after our out-of-pocket expenses have been paid."

"Whatever you say."

Juan Jose was excited entering the jet airplane. How can something this large take off and fly through the air like a bird?

He copied Jaime by snugging the belt across his waist. Jaime began asking all the travelers surrounding him if they would like to give a dollar for the chance to win it all. He was taking bets for the person who guessed the closest to the number of seconds that the lift-off takes. He quickly gathered about 10 players. Juan Jose was amazed at how easily everyone gave several hours of wages for a chance to win.

Soon the engines roared and as the jet sped down the runway Juan Jose prayed for safety and hoped the big silver bird would leap into the air since they were streaking toward the mountains. He could feel the jet pull away from the runway just as he finished his prayer. Juan Jose's knuckles were white from gripping the arms of the chair and trying to help lift the jet into the air.

A loud American with a huge stomach won the bet and everyone passed him their dollars. Juan Jose didn't understand how losing your money could be a game to be played although he had seen some of the field laborers back home after work throwing dice and passing money to each other.

Jaime, meanwhile, seemed relaxed and confident everything was going to be all right. Juan Jose's ears suddenly started crackling and popping. The flight attendant noticed his hands placed over his ears and stopped to recommend a cure.

"Try some gum," she said as she handed Juan Jose a stick of chewing gum.

He quickly popped it into his mouth and chewed it for a minute before taking it out of his mouth and halving it to place a piece in each ear.

Jaime laughed at Juan Jose while whispering, "Take it out of your ears and keep chewing it. The working of your jaws is what helps relieve the pressure."

The flight attendant soon came and asked what they would like to drink. Juan Jose ordered a cola drink and Jaime asked for a scotch and water.

"What is it that you ordered?" Juan Jose said.

"I ordered something to help me perhaps get some rest on this flight," Jaime said.

"The clouds! Look at all the clouds!" Juan Jose said to Jaime. They had broken through the white blanket and Juan Jose gasped at the puffs of white and gray stretching endlessly below.

Juan Jose thought, I can't believe my blessings for this day and that I am really flying to the United States of America to play golf.

He could not believe his eyes as he looked below at the patchwork of roads and land that made neat sections of green with brown and gray borders. As the jet approached Houston, Juan Jose saw rooftops of thousands of houses with shining blue ponds in their backyards. Jaime informed him that the ponds were called swimming pools and were made out of concrete and then filled with water so the people could swim in their own backyard.

After going through customs in Houston and changing planes, they finally arrived over Austin and Juan Jose was overwhelmed with the beauty of the rolling hills dotted with houses and swimming pools. Then he saw a magnificent green winding river and Jaime explained it to be the Colorado River that makes Lake Austin and Lady Bird Lake.

After picking Jaime's bags off of the carousel they caught a shuttle bus that took them to a remote lot to Jaime's car. They drove for 40 minutes out to an area called Lake Hideaway. Juan Jose had never seen such wealth in the construction of these houses that could have slept his entire village within their walls. He gasped as he saw Lake Travis for the first time, stretched magnificently below the hills. Sailboats skimmed over the waters. Juan Jose knew that his village was very poor compared to this part of the world and he began to feel sorry for his people for the first time ever. Juan Jose wondered why he had come to this place and if he would ever be able to look upon his village in the same way as before. Suddenly Juan Jose became sad thinking about his sister María and his niece Angelina and he realized that home is about people more than it is about places and things.

They pulled into a driveway of a house with large glass windows that enabled viewers to gaze at the beautiful lake. Juan Jose thought to himself how he never knew Jaime was so rich when he visited their tiny Honduran village.

"How can you leave this to come to Honduras to work in our village?" Juan Jose said.

"I try to follow His will and He tells me to share my gifts with others."

They sat on the balcony outdoors and watched as the sun dropped below the lake casting orange shadows across the sky and water. Jaime drank what he called a scotch with a twist but he would not let Juan Jose try one because he said the alcohol might hurt his golf. Juan Jose had fizzling water instead with a twist as he called it.

"Why is this water alive?" Juan Jose said.

"It's not alive, it's carbonated and that means there are tiny gas bubbles trying to escape."

"It tastes good. Better than the water back home."

Juan Jose was contemplative as he thought about all of the riches he had experienced compared to the bare necessities they have back home. As he looked up at the orange sunset he realized that the same sun sets upon the rich and the poor and provides a magnificent sight for both.

Jaime told him about the course he would be playing and how each round would be counted toward his qualifying to play amongst golfing professionals. Juan Jose became aware of how tired he was from the journey and told Jaime goodnight.

He kneeled in the bedroom and spent time talking to God and thanking Him for the orange sunset this evening and for the friendship of Jaime. As he finished and climbed into the bed, he sank into the mattress and realized he could not sleep on something so different from his mat on the dirt floor in his hut. He placed a blanket on the floor and lay down for the night.

Juan Jose smelled the freshly brewing coffee and stretched on the floor as he awakened to the new day. He was disoriented at first, wondering why the chickens and roosters had disappeared and forgotten to wake him. Then he remembered he was really in the United States of America and his Honduran village was so far away.

"*Buenos días, amigo*," greeted Jaime as Juan Jose entered the kitchen. "I've made coffee, but for breakfast we are going to the club for the buffet."

"What's a buffet?"

"It's a spread of all kinds of delicious things to eat and you can eat all you want."

This was incomprehensible to Juan Jose but later as they entered the club restaurant Juan Jose noticed the many tables with people eating from plates piled high with food. The waitress seated them at a table next to a fat family who took great joy in eating everything on their plates and then returning for more. Juan Jose was disturbed from this thing called a buffet. He followed Jaime through the line and took one banana for himself, one fried egg and a piece of toast. He passed mounds of bacon and ham, biscuits, salmon with cream cheese and capers, waffles, pancakes, pastries and bowls of gravy.

As they returned to their seats Juan Jose noticed Jaime's plate piled high with food. Jaime led them in a blessing of their food but Juan Jose's head remained bowed long after the "Amen."

"Are you OK?"

"No, I'm not," Juan Jose said as he lifted his head. "This is wrong."

"What's wrong?"

"I am thinking about the people of my country who do not have enough food and often no food – the children who are hungry – the children without nourishment to grow and be healthy – the thousands and thousands who die each year and those who I saw in the city getting their meals from the trash and the diseases they get from having to live that way and their lack of clean water. And here we are at a buffet with fat people eating more than they need and leaving food on their plates and water in their glasses. I vow to hunger and thirst for righteousness and to never be like these people who have too much. Food should be shared so that the unrighteousness of starvation can be helped. For if one more child is fed because of my taking less, then surely I will be filled."

5.

Blessed are the merciful, for they shall obtain mercy.

Jaime knew that the culture shock of going from a remote village in Honduras to an extravagant country club neighborhood would be difficult for Juan Jose, but he did not anticipate Juan Jose's deep emotions for what he was seeing and experiencing for the first time. After finishing breakfast it was time to take Juan Jose to the shopping mall for a wardrobe of new clothes. Juan Jose was embarrassed at all of the new clothes but Jaime convinced him that they would be needed for him to assimilate into the golfing professional community.

They left the shopping mall and headed to the golf proshop and driving range so that Juan Jose could be fitted with his own set of clubs and buy additional golfing attire.

"How can I ever repay you, Pastor Jaime? You have spent over a year's worth of my wages in just one day."

"Juan Jose, if you are as good on the course as the day in Tegucigalpa then you will repay me thousands of times over."

The golf professional named Bud headed to the range with Juan Jose and Jaime both seated in the two-row golf cart. Behind them was a massive golf bag containing a wide variety of irons and drivers to try for matching Juan Jose's swing to the perfect set of clubs.

"Jaime tells me you are the Honduran I read about in our newspaper who shot the world record 51," Bud said in fluent Spanish.

"Yes, that was my first and only time to play a course."

"I guess we'll see in a few moments," Bud said and Juan Jose didn't quite know his meaning.

Jaime said, "You will see," as they arrived at the range.

Bud handed Juan Jose a 56-degree sand wedge and told him to choose a target, tell them what he is aiming at and to take a few practice swings.

Bud's mouth dropped open as he witnessed the graceful turn and pureness of shots that all dropped within five feet of the flagstick 125 yards away.

"Amazing," Bud mumbled to himself and he handed Juan Jose a seven-iron and declared, "you need a regular lie club but with a stiff shaft because of your high clubhead speed."

Again, Juan Jose crisply struck the balls that flew at the flagstick 190 yards away.

"Can he hit a two-iron?" Bud said.

"Just as pure as a wedge," Jaime said as Bud handed the two-iron to Juan Jose.

Swish! whoosh! click, the ball sounded as it skyrocketed 250 yards away downwind and headed to the farthest flag.

"I didn't think the article was true," Bud said. "But I have seen the truth today. I am a believer."

Juan Jose said, "You are a believer *señor*? I'm glad that our *Dios* and his son Jesus are known by you."

"No, I meant a believer in your golf score. But I am a Christian believer as well."

"*Es bueno,*" said Juan Jose.

After trying several drivers Bud fitted Juan Jose with a Fire-Away brand with a large tungsten head. Bud was astounded at the way Juan Jose could fade the ball and draw the ball as instructed. Bud was as excited as Jaime at the possibilities for this Honduran golfer who seemed to have mystical powers in his golf swing.

The competition to expedite Juan Jose's earning a Professional Circuit card began the following day as the Right Technology Capital Tour was playing in Austin and hosted at the Golden Sunset Hills Country Club where Jaime was a member and a part of the golf club community where Juan Jose was staying. Since all of the available spots for the tournament were not filled, Jaime, along with Bud's help, had signed up Juan Jose to play the 18-hole qualifier and 50 golfers were vying for the three spots to compete in the Professional Circuit event at Golden Sunset Hills.

The morning started ominously with a few thunder clouds that delayed the start. Nervous golfers milled about the clubhouse and Juan Jose discovered one of the golfers named Tommy spoke some broken Spanish and they conversed.

"I heard about your 51. In fact everyone has heard about your 51," said Tommy. "My best score ever was a 64. How did you shoot such a perfect round?"

"It was not perfect," said Juan Jose. "I had a difficult time judging the slopes when flying the ball to the greens and only had one ace. Wouldn't a perfect round be without having to putt?"

"Impossible, but true. That would be a perfect game," said Tommy with a kind smile.

Juan Jose asked about Tommy's family and learned that his wife was battling breast cancer. He had three children, one-three-year old daughter and two sons ages five and seven. Tommy told him that his wife had insisted that he chase his dream of playing on the Circuit.

"I have made the decision that if I don't come home with at least $50,000, I will quit and get a real job to support my wife and family. This is the last chance I will take with their future," Tommy confided to Juan Jose.

Finally the skies cleared but the winds blew twenty to thirty miles per hour and the golfers knew they were in for a challenging day. Jaime caddied for Juan Jose and noticed the wind was making it difficult to judge where to hit the ball. However, Juan Jose's great touch around the greens had given him twelve pars and five birdies heading into the finishing hole. Even with the adversity of the wind, he was leading the round by two strokes.

The final hole was straight into the wind with water down the left side of the fairway and a narrow peninsula that held the small green surrounded on all sides by water except for the front that held deep bunkers. No one had reached the green in two all day, but Juan Jose hit a magnificent power fade that started down the water line and curved gently toward the fairway burrowing through the wind. The ball came to rest at 230 yards from the green. His two opponents playing along with him were 50 and 60 yards behind his ball. Neither had played well and seemed to be intimidated by Juan Jose's great golf skills. It didn't help that a local television station had decided to follow the threesome because of Juan Jose.

The opponents both laid up, leaving them with 100-yard approach shots to the 18th green. Jaime told Juan Jose to lay up also, because the tournament was his.

Juan Jose said, "Hand me my two-iron."

Jaime shook his head no and said, "Jaime, you are two strokes up and that is a risky shot."

Juan Jose said, "Hand me my two-iron."

Jaime again pleaded with him to hit the safe shot.

Juan Jose said, "I know I can hit the green and it will hold in the wind and sit softly near the pin."

"But if it fails and you lose the tournament, I will lose the $100,000 bet that I placed on you today to win. Half of that money is yours. You make the decision."

Juan Jose thought Jaime was teasing him about the large bet and said for the third time, "Hand me my two-iron."

Jaime reluctantly reached into the bag and gave him the two-iron. Juan Jose noticed the strange look of fear upon Jaime's worried face.

As Juan Jose addressed the ball his focus was intense. Neither the wind, the crowd, nor even Jaime existed at the moment. It was just him, the ball and the distant green as he waggled the club and drew the mental image of the ball flight to the green. His body took over as his mind calmed and with relaxed hands and arms he struck the ball perfectly, like the first time in the field back home. The ball rose into the wind and powerfully streaked toward the distant green. Soon they heard applause and yelling as the ball dropped onto the green, held by the wind and settled 10 feet from the cup.

Jaime, let out a sigh of relief and apologized for doubting the wisdom of Juan Jose's club choice. The other two golfers hit their third shots to the green and their balls were both farther away than Juan Jose's.

As Juan Jose approached the green there was a small crowd who had gathered to witness the final hole. They applauded loudly and when he realized they were clapping and hollering for him, he was embarrassed but politely removed his hat and smiled as he was instructed to do so by Jaime. It was then that he saw Dr. Julie standing in the front row of the crowd and applauding him. Their eyes met and Juan Jose nodded at her while thinking how beautiful she was dressed in pink golfing attire.

Juan Jose skimmed the leader board and noticed his name at the top. He was saddened to see Tommy's name in fourth place on the board. He was not going to achieve his dream. So close, but one stroke away.

Both of Juan Jose's opponents missed their putts, the

first rolled three feet too long and the other two feet too short. They both cleaned up the putts for par so that Juan Jose could putt for the win. Juan Jose read the uphill putt to break two feet from left to right. His stroke was pure and the ball dropped perfectly dead center for his 18th hole eagle. He had shot a remarkable 65 in a dreadful wind.

The crowd cheered loudly as Juan Jose, instructed by Jaime, removed his hat and shook the hands of his opponents. As he left the green, Dr. Julie was waiting to hug him and Jaime and congratulate the two of them. Juan Jose noticed Jaime stride over to a large man who handed Jaime a brown briefcase.

Jaime returned to Juan Jose and opened the case to show the massive stack of $100 bills.

"This is a lot of money, isn't it?" said Juan Jose.

"Yes, it is."

"Can I do whatever I wish with my share?"

"There will be much more coming your way. Certainly, it is yours to spend as you wish," Jaime said as he divided the money evenly placing his into a money bag while handing Juan Jose the brown briefcase.

Juan Jose excused himself and went into the pro shop and asked if Bud would write a note for him and provide a large envelope. Bud found an envelope and wrote as instructed. "Follow your dreams! I am praying in the name of Jesus for your wife's healing and patience and that your children will be proud of their father's persistence, determination and success. It is many years too soon to quit!"

Bud noticed Juan Jose reach into a brown briefcase and transfer many items into the envelope along with the note, but Juan Jose carefully shielded from Bud's sight the items he was placing into the envelope.

Juan Jose walked into the men's locker room and found Tommy sitting dejectedly on one of the benches. Juan Jose handed him the heavy sealed envelope and told him,

"You are not finished my friend. You were one stroke away. You will get there."

As Juan Jose walked away he smiled contentedly and thought about how much fun it was to use money to do merciful things for other people.

6.

Blessed are the pure in heart, for they shall see God.

Juan Jose entered the weekend tournament as one of the three players who earned a spot in the qualifier. During the next four rounds he shot 64, 66, 67 and finished with a 63. The crowds grew each day to watch the "Peasant Phenom" as the media named the quiet man from the Olancho Region of Honduras. The second place golfer was at 14 under par – a far distance from Juan Jose's -28.

Between Jaime's side bets with the gambling crowd and the actual winnings of the tournament, Juan Jose's earnings were significant. On Sunday, after the tournament, Juan Jose attended Jaime's evening worship service. Dr. Julie sat next to him and as she touched him gently on the arm and squeezed while congratulating him, her touch warmed his heart.

"Jaime asked me to come over for dinner tonight to celebrate your victory," she whispered in fluent Spanish.

"That will be great," Juan Jose said in English.

Julie wondered how Juan Jose had learned so much English in just a few days' time.

Jaime's sermon spoke about one of The Beatitudes and how being pure in heart enables one to see God. Juan Jose was awed by the beauty of the church and could not keep from staring at the scenes of Jesus depicted in the beautiful stained glass windows. The choir sang a magnificent gospel song accompanied on a baby grand piano and Juan Jose couldn't believe how different this was from the small pole barn church constructed in his village – and yet, God was equally present in both locations.

After the service, Jaime picked up some delicious barbecue, beans, cole slaw, potato salad, onions and dill pickles from his favorite place called Franky Ken's and they set up to serve on Jaime's patio overlooking the hill country and Lake Travis in the distance. Dr. Julie knocked on the door a short time later and they all conversed in Spanish about the golf tournament and the sermon while enjoying each other's company.

Juan Jose said, "Jaime, do you think it would be possible for me to earn enough money playing golf to build a hospital in our valley back home? I have been asking God what am I doing here, and how can I glorify Him?"

Dr. Julie said, "What an amazing idea. You have such spiritual depth. I believe that is your real talent. Golf is just a means for your pure heart to be manifested."

Jaime said, "It will cost millions of dollars to buy land and build a hospital, but I'm not saying that it wouldn't be worth it and save many lives. Is this something you believe God is calling you to do?"

"Yes, I have spent many hours in prayer since the first day that you handed me so much money."

"If you are so blessed to keep winning, your dream will come true. I have been working on a sponsor's exemption for you to play against the finest golfers in the world at the Royal Lochs Links. It is the host of a major tournament in just a few weeks. The world needs a hero right now, Juan Jose, and perhaps you are the one. The media is in a frenzy over your 51 score and winning the tournament today. I am having a difficult time keeping them away from you."

"I am a simple peasant who cut the fields. I am no hero."

Dr. Julie jumped back into the conversation, "But God chooses ordinary people to accomplish extraordinary things and sometimes they are the most unlikely candidates. Moses and Paul immediately come to mind."

"I will continue to pray," said Juan Jose.

"As will I," said Julie.

"As will I," said Jaime.

After dinner, Jaime excused himself to put away the food and as Julie and Juan Jose tried to help him, Jaime insisted that the two of them sit and enjoy the full moon rising over the lake.

"That is magnificent," Juan Jose declared. "I am glad to see the moon shining so brightly because the stars are mostly missing."

"What do you mean, the stars are mostly missing?" said Julie.

"Ever since I've been here, I have noticed that instead of seeing millions of stars in the sky like back home, that there are only a few hundred. I wonder where they went?"

"The stars are still there in the sky but all of the city lights keep them from being seen because of what we call light pollution."

"I very much enjoy the light in the house but I'm not sure it is worth it - especially if it takes away the stars. Even things that appear to be all good can have some bad mixed in."

"Kind of like people," Julie said softly. "You probably think I'm a saint after saving those babies, but I am not."

"Why do you say that?"

"Because I was married to a developer who built many of these homes and many others in remote and beautiful places and now we hate each other. I'm not sure that I can fall in love again. It was too painful and I feel broken and confused."

"What caused you to stop loving him?"

"I came home when a plane trip to a conference was cancelled because of terrible weather. I stopped by a store and bought an expensive bottle of wine and when I saw his car at home in the driveway I sneaked in quietly to surprise him. The surprise was hugely on me when I found him wrapped in the arms of his secretary in our bed."

"He is a fool. How could he do that to a woman as beautiful and nice as you?"

"You are a sweet man with a pure heart."

Jaime returned and interrupted the moment asking, "Have you two been mesmerized by the moon?"

"Julie was telling me about love pollution… I mean light pollution and how the lights from the city cause many of the stars to be unseen in the sky. I miss them greatly because they can chase the darkness from my mood just by staring at their twinkling lights."

Julie said, "I was telling him about love pollution too and how my ex-husband Stephen pretty much extinguished my lights of love."

Jaime said, "I know you are still reeling, but I pray for eventual healing."

Juan Jose said, "I will pray that you move away from your darkness and back to the twinkling lights of love."

"You two are both kind and gentle. Why didn't I find either of you before finding Stephen?"

"But you have found us," said Juan Jose.

"Tell me, how do I see God in my failed marriage? Sometimes, I blame Him when things don't go right."

Juan Jose said simply, "I have learned to be content when I am hungry and when I am well fed. This is how I am able to see God always."

"I couldn't have said that any better and I went to seminary," said Jaime. "Amen and amen."

7.

Blessed are the peacemakers, for they shall be called children of God.

Juan Jose spent his time leading up to the Scottish tournament inundated in his Bible and he continued memorizing verse after verse. Alongside his Spanish version he would read the same passage in an English version and was quickly becoming proficient in English.

He continued to think about Dr. Moss, dreaming that he could hold her in his arms and restore her brokenness. The day of the flight to Edinburgh she volunteered to take them to the airport to wish he and Jaime good luck and she hugged them and kissed them both on their cheeks.

"I want to see you holding the Royal Loch Links Trophy at the end of the tournament," said Julie. "Bring it back for me to see."

"What is the Royal Loch Links trophy?"

"It is the historical trophy awarded to the winner of the tournament each year," said Jaime. "The current trophy has been used since 1922 and everyone who wins has his name engraved on it and gets to keep it for a year before returning it for a replica to keep forever."

"I will try and win it for you to see."

Juan Jose mostly slept and prayed on the long flight across the ocean. Finally they arrived in Edinburgh and rented a car to head up the Scottish coast to Royal Loch. They checked into the Royal Loch Inn consisting of two old adjoining castles just a few hundred yards away from the course where the tournament would be played. Juan Jose was somewhat awestruck to learn that golf had originated in Scotland some six hundred years ago.

They arrived on Sunday which would give Juan Jose three days to practice links golf and get used to the intricacies of playing golf in the wind with gorse bushes, pot bunkers and deep rough to avoid. Juan Jose would play the Loch Winds Course on Monday, The Royal Loch Links Course on Tuesday and then rest up for the tournament and practice his short game on Wednesday.

After breakfast they arrived on the first tee of Loch Winds appropriately named for the winds howling through the inlet. Loch Winds stands between the loch and the Royal Loch Links' Clubhouse and Jaime knew it would provide an ultimate test of tricky sloped and fast greens, uneven fairways, heavy gorse and a lot of bunkers. The yardage book with actual aerials and hints of how to play each hole was carried by Jaime. Juan Jose and Jaime had to ask a special favor to be paired with a couple of locals George McDougal and Craig McReynolds who would provide advice throughout the round. The Scots traditionally will let a twosome go alone if they don't know the twosome behind them.

Jaime placed a large wager with George and Craig that Juan Jose would shoot par or better on his first time to play a links course. Even though they recognized Juan Jose as the Honduran shown on TV who had the world record low score and would be playing in the Royal Loch Links Tournament, they doubted he could master the mystery of Scottish golf on his first time out. Standing on the first tee and watching Juan Jose's ball ripping through the wind in a perfect line between the two fairway bunkers hanging nearer the right one made George and Craig think they had probably already lost the wager. Juan Jose's powerful drive left him a 67-yard shot to the green.

Over the course of the round, Juan Jose learned to hit low burrowing shots into the wind. He learned the running punch shot and how to putt from well off the green to eliminate the wind. He intentionally hit into the sand and mastered the huge deep bunkers near the greens with a 64 degree wedge. At the end of the 6,746 yards from the back tees, Juan Jose had equaled the par 71. He had twelve pars, three birdies and three bogeys. It was the first time he had ever made bogey by three-putting two of the greens and having to lay up out of one of the fairway bunkers and two-putting the green for a bogey.

"Yer one smooth Honduran golfer," said Craig as he peeled money from his wallet and handed it to Jaime. "I'll be placing a wager on ye to win the tournament and get our money back. Been a real pleasure watching ye strike the ball. Yer on the way to greatness."

"I am trying to win enough money to buy land for a hospital in my valley in Honduras," said Juan Jose.

"Well, we just made a donation to yer personal mission. At least it's going to a good cause," said George. "Best of luck to ye. May the wind be at yer back during the tourney."

Juan Jose and Jaime played The Royal Loch Links Course on Tuesday alone at their request and used the round to pick landing areas and make extensive notes for preferred distances for approach shots in preparation for the tournament. Juan Jose smiled as he walked the old golf course and he thought about how many golfers have traversed the same track over the last several hundred years. Several times during the round he found himself in a dreamlike state thinking that he had been here before with true déjà vu moments. The rain moved in halfway through the round and he learned how to hit the ball with rain gloves and donned a waterproof rain suit. The rain reminded him of the rainy season back home in Honduras. Hondurans in his home valley don't hurry to get out of the rain because they know the day will be wet and in order to get something done it will require getting soaked. Juan Jose approached this round the same although it was a tough round in the elements and he finished at two over par. Jaime shot a 101.

On Wednesday, Juan Jose practiced bunker shots, punch shots and putting all distances including running the ball up from beyond the green. The rest of the afternoon he spent resting in the Royal Loch Inn and studying his Bible. Jaime could not keep the media at bay any longer and an American reporter caught up with them in the lobby of the hotel as they were heading to dinner.

"Juan Jose, do you think you have a chance to win the tournament?" questioned the news reporter.

"I need to win," said Juan Jose sincerely.

"So, you are predicting a victory," the reporter tried to lead him into sounding arrogant.

Jaime jumped into the interview trying to deflect the tone, "Juan Jose has a goal to build a hospital back home. He knows the better he finishes, the closer he will come to making his dream come true."

"Tell us about yourself," said the reporter.

"I am a Christian who loves my Creator and I try to serve Him humbly. Just a few months ago I was cutting the landowner's fields and now I am taking divots with golf clubs. God has equipped me to work for His Kingdom and I am just walking daily where He leads me."

Jaime interrupted, "Thank you for speaking with us, and if you'll excuse us, Juan Jose must eat dinner and rest up for his early tee time."

Juan Jose ate an appetizer, drank water for his meal and headed back to his hotel room where he prayed for God to lead him toward his goal of building a hospital in his valley back home. He slept peacefully and the mattress was firm enough that he chose not to sleep on the floor. He was dreaming of waterfalls and that his body was flying above the valley and that he could adjust the height of his flight with his arms and mind. The knocking on his door startled him awake as Jaime declared, "Let's go win this major tournament!"

The morning was glorious and an unusually blue sky day for the Scotland coast. The day would yield some low rounds and Juan Jose carded a 66 just two strokes off the lead of 64. He might have been the leader if he hadn't hit out-of-bounds on the Rabbit Hole 12th by taking the ball too far over the building to the right and working his draw, but just not quite enough for the line he had chosen. He noted the mistake and vowed that on the next three rounds he would start the ball a bit further left and hold the line.

After the first round, the media was abuzz about the Honduran novice who was two strokes off the lead. The Scots always pick up on the underdog and the crowds flocked to follow Juan Jose as he was paired with the leading money winner on the tour – Timmy Gunn. The second day he carded another 66 as the weather held and his opponent stayed in the lead carding a 65 with a three stroke lead over Juan Jose heading into Saturday's round. The weather turned on Saturday and the wind howled as the scores climbed. Balls were vibrating on the speedy greens in the wind and Juan Jose had to smile extra long to concentrate before making a putting stroke. At the end of the day he had stayed three strokes back of Timmy Gunn with both golfers carding 68s. The closest score from the rest of the field was Rodney Farrell just four strokes back, just one behind Juan Jose, and then a pack of five golfers who stood at twelve under par, seven strokes off the lead. Sunday would be a great finish and the crowds swelled to follow Juan Jose and Timmy Gunn. The morning was overcast and rain was predicted for later in the day. A special fan had flown from the U.S. just to be there on Sunday because she had a special feeling that this was going to be Juan Jose's finest moment.

Finally after a long warm up on the range and putting green, the announcer declared, "From the Agalta Valley in the Olancho Region of Honduras, first time Royal Loch Links Tournament player Juan Jose Delgado."

The crowd cheered loudly and Juan Jose smiled with joy as he approached the tee box and deftly inserted his tee and started his pre-shot routine. The opening hole is 382 yards and the only trouble is the winding creek, or burn as it is called in Scotland, that traverses the fairway to within five yards to the front of the green. Juan Jose hit a beautiful drive with a slight draw that rolled out to 325 yards leaving a 57-yard shot to the narrow green.

The announcer said, "From Johannesburg, South Africa, and leader of the 152nd Royal Loch Links Tournament, Timmy Gunn."

The crowd cheered but not as loudly as they had for Juan Jose as Timmy began his routine and smacked his three-wood 256 yards to leave a full shot to the flag in the middle of the green. He hit his wedge carrying past the flag and spun the ball back toward the hole. The crowd applauded his shot that left the ball 10 feet from the cup.

Juan Jose knew he wanted to hit a high shot directly toward the pin. He slightly opened the face of his lob wedge and hit a magnificent shot that fell from the sky toward the pin and stuck where it hit four feet from the cup.

Timmy just missed his 10 footer that lipped out and Juan Jose served notice with a birdie putt to close within two strokes of Timmy's lead. Jaime, who was caddying for Juan Jose, gave him a fist bump and encouraged him saying,

"If you birdie them all we'll be building a hospital."

The second hole named Howling was playing 462 yards and the key was to drive the ball as close to Doyle's bunker on the left since the flag was placed far to the right side of the green. A slight fade on the second shot with an iron would carry the green's ridge and feed nicely to the hole.

Juan Jose played the ball to draw from the middle of the fairway and to take Doyle's bunker out of play by rolling the ball well past it. The mighty drive turned over and rolled back to left center of the fairway 25 yards beyond the bunker and 115 yards to the pin.

Timmy also played a draw but his ball barely missed Doyle's bunker and he had a 135-yard shot to the green. His approach shot faded gently toward the hole and rolled to within six feet of the pin.

Juan Jose played his sand wedge with a three-quarter swing and placed the ball five feet from the pin. Both golfers made their birdie putts as the crowd roared its approval.

The leaders moved on to the third hole named Shaman (Out). At Royal Loch Links Course there are holes with the same names on the front nine and back nine which are designated "Out" on the front and "In" on the back. Shaman (Out) was playing 406 yards and the left side is favored although pot bunkers and gorse are lurking if the ball draws too much for the right-handed golfer.

Juan Jose drove a perfectly straight ball down the fairway that left an easy 100-yard shot to the green. Timmy's drive turned over a little too much from right to left and put him having to take the ball over the teardrop-shaped bunker protecting the left of the green. Timmy chose his wedge to play his shot into the green and hit on the left side to let the ball roll downward toward the hole on the left-to-right slope of the green. The ball gained speed on the slope and rolled 12 feet past the pin. Juan Jose again played a three-quarter sand wedge past the pin and let the ball trickle back to the hole where it stopped three feet from the cup.

The crowd cheered and applauded the masterful shot.

Although Timmy was starting to feel the pressure of high stakes championship golf, he had been there many times and knew the right thoughts to calm his nerves. He breathed in deeply as he addressed his putt and lined up meticulously for a three-foot side break. His twelve-footer nestled solidly in the cup as the crowd boomed its approval. Juan Jose calmly stroked his short putt perfectly into the hole and remained two strokes back.

On the fourth hole called Kite Kilter (Out) a brisk wind began to blow. Either side of the fairway would work but the right side provided a better look at the approach to the green. A huge mound on the left in front of the green obscured the pin. Juan Jose bombed a 300-yard drive down the right side as he turned his ball from left-to-right expertly working the wind with a power fade and left himself 180 yards to the green. Timmy Gunn's drive was about 20 yards short of Juan Jose's and he hit a five-iron to the green as the ball scooted across the green and found the big bunker behind the green. Juan Jose calmly took his eight-iron and rode the wind to the green, leaving himself a 20-foot putt. The deep bunker gave Timmy no chance at par as he had to hit the ball very high just to clear the lip. He was left with a 35-foot putt and he almost made the impossible par but the ball just caught the lip of the hole and rolled three feet away. Juan Jose miraculously made his 20-foot putt as the howling wind pushed the ball onto the line and into the cup. Juan Jose left the green tied with the great Timmy Gunn.

The wind strengthened and a heavy mist enveloped the course as the field fell away from the leaders. The closest golfer to Delgado and Gunn was Artur Santos from Brazil and he was four strokes away, in the clubhouse, having accomplished his two below par for the day before the weather turned foul.

Juan Jose and Timmy played holes five through twelve even with six pars, one birdie and one bogey apiece which was a remarkable feat in the adverse weather conditions.

Jaime walked alongside Juan Jose to the 13th hole and whispered, "Six holes to go, my friend. It's time to move away from the competition. Think for one moment about the hospital we will build in your valley. Picture the sick children being healed and the mothers and fathers who will be saved from an early death because God has led you to this destination today."

Juan Jose looked into the eyes of Jaime and declared, "I will not fail."

The fans following the leaders and walking the five of the last six holes were treated to an amazing display of concentration and skill as Juan Jose birdied Kite Kilter (In), Gruff Grouse (In), and Soaring Sandwich Tern (In) and had pars on the other two, while, Timmy Gunn, who was not giving in, birdied for himself Long Link (In), Downward Dyke (In) and Soaring Sandwich Tern (In). Juan Jose and Timmy remained tied heading to the final hole.

Jaime whispered to Juan Jose, "How are you dealing with the pressure? Is there anything I can do to help you?"

Juan Jose said, "Pressure is having nothing to eat or to bring to your family. Pressure is having a sick baby with no one with the skills to help. Pressure is not having work to do. I have no pressure this day or on this final hole."

Timmy stepped to the tee box of the 18th named Deep Divots (In) and played his three-wood downwind and left a 100-yard shot over The Rocks of Wrath to hopefully get up and down for a winning birdie. Juan Jose asked Jaime to hand him the driver. He knew the wind would give him the chance to drive the green. Juan Jose smiled to find all of the joy in the swinging of the club. The ball rocketed off the tee as the crowd surrounding the tee box roared its approval. The ball came to rest just past the Rocks of Wrath about 80 feet short of the hole in a small valley in front of the green.

Juan Jose and Jaime strode down the fairway behind Timmy and his caddie and stopped 10 yards back and off to the right side as Timmy took the sand wedge that he hoped would lead him to victory. His three-quarter swing with the wedge was simple and pure as the ball rode the wind toward the flag and the cup, landing just a couple of feet short with just enough spin to back up only a foot, leaving a three-foot birdie attempt.

Jaime looked at Juan Jose and Juan Jose noticed the fear in Jaime's eyes. Juan Jose intensely stared back and then laughed to release the tension. "Fear not," Juan Jose said confidently.

As the two golfers and their caddies approached the 18th green, the swelling crowd applauded thunderously the tournament record low scores of Gunn and Delgado. Both golfers tipped their caps to show respect to the crowd.

Juan Jose felt the fierce wind at his back and asked for his seven-iron to run the ball through the slight valley and onto the green feeling that the wind was too strong to throw the ball into the air. He walked to the hole and noticed all of the undulation and treacherous path to the hole. He needed a sign that this decision was the right one and at just that moment he thought about Julie Moss and her telling him to bring home the Royal Loch Links Trophy. He had no idea that Julie was standing just off the green amongst the crowd and had traveled to Scotland when she knew that he had a chance to win the tournament. Juan Jose looked her direction and although he couldn't see her, he felt the love and encouragement of the crowd. He walked back to his ball and took two practice swings staring intently while imagining the ball rolling up the valley onto the green, breaking right-to-left in a six-foot curve and settling into the hole 80 feet away. The gallery of people held its breath as the wind howled. Then Juan Jose struck the ball and it rose through the valley up onto the green. The crowd anticipated the greatness of the shot and shouts began to ring out as it traveled over the green 50 feet, 40 feet, 30 feet, 20 feet, 10 feet then the final curve toward the hole – straight toward the hole and plunked into the cup after striking the pin dead center.

The crowd went crazy with screaming and applause. Jaime leaped into the air again and again. Juan Jose dropped to his knees, closed his eyes and prayed, "*Gracias Dios,*" then rose and removed his hat walking toward Timmy Gunn with outstretched hand.

"That was the most magnificent bump-and-run that I've ever seen. Congratulations!" said Timmy.

After Timmy completed his birdie putt, Juan Jose again shook Timmy's hand declaring humbly, "It was my pleasure to play with a great golfer."

With amazement, Juan Jose noticed the beautiful blonde running across the green and leaping into his arms as she planted a kiss on his lips with tears of joy in her eyes.

"Julie! What are you doing here?"

"Watching, my hero win the Royal Loch Links Tournament!" she yelled, and kissed him again.

Back in the United States, another man who knew Julie watched jealously as his former wife, whom he had cheated on for an adulterous relationship with his secretary, kissed the lips of another with the entire world watching the tournament to see. He listened intently to the brief interview just off the green that was televised and what Juan Jose told the announcer about using his winnings to buy the land to build a hospital in the Agalta Valley.

Jaime, Julie and Juan Jose had a celebratory dinner in the hotel after Juan Jose signed autograph after autograph for his admirers. The media was abuzz about the great victory from the miraculous Honduran man who had learned to play golf in the same year as winning at Royal Loch Links.

Juan Jose traveled back to the valley with Jaime to purchase the land for the hospital. As they went to close the deal with the landowner, Pablo Rosario, they were surprised to find that he had sold the land that morning to a man named Stephen Moss, Julie's former husband, the developer. Jaime was furious and berated the land owner for selling the land out from under them.

"How could you go back on the deal you made with us?"

Juan Jose spoke up, "Please, don't blame Pablo for taking more money for the land. He has a family to take care of, and why shouldn't he do the best that he can?"

Pablo said, "I'm sorry Jaime and Juan Jose. It is just that he offered so much more."

"It is not a problem, don't think any more about it," said Juan Jose.

As they left the landowner's office there was a great commotion down the street. Pistols had been drawn and there was shouting and great tension as the dangerous conflict was igniting.

Juan Jose ran down the street and saw pistols pointed at an *Americano*. He had a guess that the man who had made a pass at one of the Honduran's wife was Stephen Moss.

Juan Jose shouted, *"Paren hombres, que paso?"*

The village men began to explain what had happened.

Juan Jose diffused the situation by making Stephen Moss apologize and the men lowered their pistols.

Stephen thought that this Honduran who saved him looked familiar and his face showed shock as Juan Jose introduced himself, "I am Juan Jose Delgado."

Stephen muttered, "I am Stephen Moss."

"I know," said Juan Jose. "You are Dr. Julie's former husband and you bought the land that I wanted for the hospital."

"Then why did you save my life?"

"Because killing brings more killing. And I have already forgiven you for buying the land."

"Why?"

"Because, Julie once loved you, and I know that you have goodness within you, if she fell in love with you and married you."

Stephen felt a pang of remorse come over him. How could this simple Honduran man reach out and touch his darkened soul and offer a glimmer of light to enter back in?

"I will sell you the land back and make a donation toward the hospital," Stephen said emotionally, knowing he was crossing the divide from evil back to good.

"Deal," said Juan Jose.

Jaime was amazed at all he had just witnessed as he whispered, "Blessed is this peacemaker, for he shall be called a son of God."

8.

Blessed are those who have been persecuted for righteousness' sake, for theirs is the Kingdom of Heaven. Blessed are you when people reproach you, persecute you, and say all kinds of evil against you falsely, for my sake. Rejoice and be exceedingly glad, for great is your reward in heaven. For that is how they persecuted the prophets who were before you.

The media fed the frenzy that became known as Juan Jose mania. After the Royal Loch Links Tournament, Juan Jose played two of the circuit tournaments leading up to the Pro Championship and won both by more than ten strokes.

The media also reported how all of his winnings were going to be spent on a hospital in his home valley and that he would retire after playing the Pro Championship. This win would allow him to reach the monetary goal to build the new hospital. Of course, because of his simple persona and bold endorsements of Christianity, and how it changes lives, there were many skeptical people who made fun of him and wished for his failure. Labels like "Jesus Freak" and "Holy Golf Ball Roller" were cruelly spouted by those who didn't embrace the goodness, truth and mercy that Juan Jose stood for.

Jaime secretly bet all that there was on the Pro Championship tournament to be played at Dazzling Dunes, trying to leverage the money to multiply many-fold for the last tournament golf for Juan Jose. Unbeknownst to Juan Jose, more than fifty million dollars was at stake.

Since announcing this was his last tournament and that he was going back home to start a hospital and live the rest of his life helping his people in the Olancho Region, the vast public opinion was that it was a shame that such a talent would be wasted. Most of the world turned against him as the media played on the turmoil of his quitting the Professional Circuit.

Juan Jose longed for the days to be spent with his niece Angelina, his sister María and the people back home. Although he loved Dr. Julie Moss and enjoyed the moments spent with her, he knew she could never live in the valley and be content with the simple life. In fact, Juan Jose had become a friend of Stephen Moss and continued to mentor him, leading him to accept Christ, and he was helping him to reconcile his relationship with Julie. Juan Jose knew that Stephen was a changed and forgiven man, completely different than the one who had committed adultery.

Dazzling Dunes, fronting a three-mile stretch of Lake Huron, was set up to play extremely difficult for the tournament and would demand the supreme test of all of the professionals' skills over the course of 7,813 yards containing somewhere near 800 bunkers.

Juan Jose and Jaime arrived early to prepare by playing practice rounds, just as they had before the Royal Loch

Links Tournament. Juan Jose appeared to be on his game as usual by shooting four under par on both practice rounds. Juan Jose was impressed with the intricate design of the course.

On the first three days of the tournament Juan Jose was steady with his game and surged into the lead shooting 67, 68 and 70 for an 11 under lead with the next closest golfer, Lou Carter at eight under, just three shots back. Jaime felt much relieved heading into the final round with a three-stroke margin knowing all of the money that was at stake.

After playing nine holes of his final round, Juan Jose had picked up a stroke on Lou Carter and no one else was close. Then the inevitable happened, as all golfers who have ever played the game know so well – the wheels started to come off. Unexplainable and incomprehensible it was to Juan Jose and especially to Jaime. Those afraid of all of the goodness that Juan Jose represented cheered his sudden humanness heading towards failure.

It started on the tenth hole named Veracity, the shortest par four on the course. Juan Jose attempted to drive the green but the ball did not turn over and flew straight into a deep bunker to the right of the green. His sand shot just caught the lip of the bunker and came up 30 feet short of the cup. Lou Carter had hit a safe shot to leave a 100-yard approach which he had struck to within five feet of the pin.

Juan Jose envisioned the path of his putt and the speed to drop the ball safely into the cup. He replaced his ball marker with his ball and as he approached the ball to make the putt he noticed a small bug crawling over the top of his ball, so he backed up, replaced his ball with a mark and blew the bug off the ball. It was enough of a break in his routine to distract his concentration and as he replaced the mark with the ball and readdressed the ball with his putter, he could not remember the exact line envisioned for his putt. He contemplated and picked what he thought he remembered as the spot to run the ball to let it feed to the hole, but he was mistaken about the mark and the ball missed by two feet and ran three feet past the hole.

Lou Carter putted and made the five-foot birdie dead center of the cup. Juan Jose knew that he must confidently make the par and he putted the ball firmly aiming to take a half ball outside the cup break. The ball defied gravity, or at least appeared to do so, and instead of falling into the hole, it lipped out. Bogey! Two of his four-stroke lead had disappeared.

Jaime tried to calm his own nerves by telling Juan Jose, "No problem. You will get them back over the next hole or two and you still have the lead. Don't worry."

Juan Jose could hear an unusual amount of tension in Jaime's voice. Even though he spoke confident words, there was fear in his voice and it made Juan Jose wonder where the fear was coming from.

The leaders moved on to Sullen Sands, the extra-long par five 11th hole. Lou hit a booming drive down the center of the fairway. Juan Jose's drive flew right for some inexplicable reason. For the first time, he didn't understand why his ball didn't go along his envisioned path. Something had broken just a little in his swing and he was helpless to know what. It was just enough to put doubt into his mind as he approached the ball in the deep sand trap to the right of the fairway. All he could do was swing mightily and get a wedge on the ball to advance the ball back into the short grass. Lou placed a perfect three-wood for an easy pitch to the green. Juan Jose wanted to stay aggressive and to hit his three-iron to the green.

Jaime questioned his club choice, "Why not lay up in three and get up and down for par. I will bet you could stay even with Lou. I still don't think he'll get up and down for birdie."

Juan Jose said, "Three-iron, please," but the doubt

and fear of Jaime was starting to have a negative effect on Juan Jose. Just before he hit the three-iron he wondered if he should have listened to Jaime. The iron struck the ball solidly but the adrenaline behind the shot sent the ball all the way to the bunker behind the green.

Lou pitched his ball to within 10 feet for an excellent look at another birdie and Juan Jose hit his sand shot perfectly on line but it stopped two feet short of the hole. Lou made a beautiful putt to the hole and birdied while Juan Jose made his par and lost another stroke of the lead. "Mo" had jumped off of Juan Jose's back and onto Lou's as the momentum clearly had shifted on the final nine holes.

Lou surveyed the 12th hole par three called Dime. The small green seemed to rise up from the many bunkers surrounding it with the lake off to the left. He made a pure swing and placed the ball neatly five feet from the cup.

Juan Jose asked for his nine-iron and Jaime insisted he hit the eight because of the wind. The hole was playing 163 yards and Juan Jose again overcooked the shot and it flew into the back bunker. The nine-iron would have been the right club with the kind of shot that he hit.

Jaime apologized, "I'm sorry my friend. No more advice from me."

"No need to apologize. I listened and chose the club."

Juan Jose made a fine sand shot but left the ball a foot from the hole. Lou made his five-footer for another birdie and the Pro Championship was now tied as Juan Jose tapped in for par.

Lou surveyed the fairway of Water's Ledge and expertly drove his ball down the right side and avoided the awkward lies and cliff to the left. Juan Jose's ball started to draw instead of fade and found a small sand dune with the ball well above his feet. Jaime became more and more distraught and his sagging shoulders were noticed by Juan Jose as he walked down the fairway.

Juan Jose wondered why Jaime seemed to be so tense and said, "I will try my best to win, but if we come in second we will still build a hospital."

Jaime said, "We really need to win."

Juan Jose asked for his eight-iron and aimed just to the rightside of the green toward the back bunker, knowing that the slope would make his ball go right to left. The ball was well played and came to rest 12 feet from the cup.

Lou hit his wedge to within six feet.

Juan Jose confidently surveyed the green, aligned his putt, stroked the ball and missed!

Lou made another birdie and left the green with a lead for the first time during the tournament.

Over the next holes named Bewitched, Lovely, Sandy Save and Hammer, Juan Jose lost another two strokes to Lou. People watching the tournament and even the announcers called it a meltdown as the Royal Loch Links Tournament Champion turned into the Pro Championship goat, ready for slaughter. Many people rejoiced that the Honduran novice had come back to earth and was failing. Some skeptics and atheists were saying that his God wasn't big enough to keep him winning.

On the 18th and final hole named Doubting, Lou safely drove his ball down the right side to leave a long iron to the hole as he was protecting his three-stroke lead. Juan Jose let it all out going with the driver to the left with a 300-plus-yard carry over dunes and bunkers to leave a shorter approach shot. Lou hit his four-iron to the green and left himself a 20-foot putt.

Juan Jose knew this would be his last professional golf shot as he calmly asked Jaime for his nine iron. His journey flashed before him – from field laborer to professional golfer and now soon to be a hospital builder. He prayed thanks to God and gripped his nine-iron and made one last miraculous shot – he knocked the ball into the hole for an eagle. The crowd went crazy shouting, "Juan Jose, Juan Jose, Juan Jose!" The applause was deafening as the two golfers approached the green. After Lou two-putted to win by a stroke, the crowd again applauded long and loud for both Juan Jose and Lou. Juan Jose congratulated Lou and noticed that Jaime had left the green. The announcers asked Juan Jose if he had changed his mind about returning to his valley to build a hospital and give up his golf career. Juan Jose assured them that this was his discernment of what God wanted him to do. The doubters called him foolish, an uneducated idiot and a great waste of talent.

Juan Jose caught up with a depressed Jaime in the clubhouse and said, "Why so glum, my friend?"

Jaime could not bear to confess that he had lost all of their money. He said, "I'm just sad that this is the last time I get to caddie for you."

"Yes, but there is much greater good to accomplish in the Agalta Valley."

"I know that we both have tickets to leave tomorrow, but I'm going to have to come later."

Jaime slept terribly that night and Juan Jose slept peacefully. Jaime looked awful with large black circles beneath his bloodshot eyes from a fitful night as he drove Juan Jose to the early morning flight. They hugged each other behind the car as Juan Jose gathered his luggage.

"See you soon, my friend," said Juan Jose.

"*Adiós amigo,*" said Jaime. Little did he know his goodbye would be a farewell.

The plane lost an engine during the landing descent into Tegucigalpa – one of the world's toughest landings for a pilot. The mechanical failure combined with the strong wind from a storm was enough to cause the jet to crash just past the runway as it spiraled out of control. There were only two survivors – a mother and her young baby. She told the news media about the Honduran man who introduced himself as Juan Jose when he sat down, and how he had laid his hands on her baby daughter named Hope and helped hold Hope tightly to her lap during the crash. She described feeling like a supernatural protective shield radiated from his hands to all around them as he prayed intensely for them to be saved in those moments of terror.

The world mourned as the news spread across the planet. Jaime, Julie and Stephen Moss hugged each other and cried openly as their sadness tore through their souls. Jaime met with the media later in the day and told how he had lost everything that Juan Jose had won. His soul was tormented and he said he realized he was obsessed with gambling and would quit this day and forevermore to honor the memory of his friend Juan Jose. Jaime reminded the broadcast team of Juan Jose's dream of building the hospital and how he had failed Juan Jose. Jaime was completely devastated.

The next day, after Jaime conducted a memorial service in the U.S., the miracle began to happen. Checks from all over the world began pouring into an account that had been established by a group of Christian touring professionals who had also spent their pooled money on an immediate social media blitz to raise funds for Juan Jose's hospital. Millions and millions of dollars appeared and no one wrote a larger check than Stephen Moss who credited Juan Jose with not only helping reconcile his relationship with Julie but also with saving his soul through teaching him the truth of the Gospel of Jesus Christ.

Today, in the middle of the Agalta Valley there is a modern fully staffed hospital healing people and saving lives. Everyone who comes to the hospital notices the huge bronze statue out front of a Honduran man holding his niece Angelina in one arm and who props a golf club driver upon the ground with his other. The inscription at the base of the sculpture, which was Pastor Jaime's idea, reads:

Blessed are the poor in spirit,
for theirs is the Kingdom of Heaven.

Blessed are those who mourn,
for they shall be comforted.

Blessed are the gentle,
for they shall inherit the earth.

Blessed are those who hunger and thirst after righteousness,
for they shall be filled.

Blessed are the merciful,
for they shall obtain mercy.

Blessed are the pure in heart,
for they shall see God.

Blessed are the peacemakers,
for they shall be called children of God.

Blessed are those who have been persecuted for righteousness'
sake, for theirs is the Kingdom of Heaven.

Blessed are you when people reproach you, persecute you,
and say all kinds of evil against you falsely, for my sake.
Rejoice, and be execeedingly glad, for great is your reward
in heaven. For that is how they persecuted the prophets who
were before you.

Denouement

The hospital door opens and the early morning light
illuminates the new day with golden hues streaked through
the early fog hung below the mountaintops. A huge man in

a wheelchair slowly rolls his way across the stone plaza over to the radiant statue of Juan Jose and Angelina. The man's legs are heavily bandaged and crushed from the tree that fell across him in the terrible logging accident as the chain saw swiped across one leg spewing his life blood up into the air and over the ground. The man knows he would have died if not for the Juan Jose Delgado Memorial Hospital recently opened in the valley and the staff who saved his life.

Tim Bigelow gazes upward at the bronze face of Juan Jose shadowed by the clouds and remembers striking him and firing him that day when Juan Jose refused to cut the trees in the old-growth pine forest. Since the accident, Tim has learned about the Gospel of Jesus Christ after intently studying the Spanish language Bible that he found on the table in his hospital room that was provided by Pastor Jaime's church in Austin, Texas. Tim was amazed to learn about Saul of Taurus who persecuted the Christians and was blinded on the road to Damascus. He studied this man named Saul whose heart was changed and who became Paul, an ardent follower of Christ.

Tim bowed his head in prayer and said, "Father God, thank You for Your amazing grace and forgiveness of my past, and thank You, for this man Juan Jose, who brought this hospital to our valley. When I walk again, take my feet and lead them to who You want me to meet. Have me do what You want me to do and say what You want me say, and then Lord let me just get out of Your way. Amen."

Tim lifted his head and as he gazed upward again at the bronze statue, the sunlight passed through the moving clouds and lifting fog in just such a way that Juan Jose's slight smile and mouth were illuminated as a beautiful red dragonfly touched down to pause on Juan Jose's lips. Tim wept in awe of God's communication and creation unfolding in the world around him.

Afterword

While this book is fiction, the Olancho Region and the Agalta Valley are real places in Honduras and HOI has been sending mission teams to Rancho El Paraíso for more than twenty years. Thousands of church members from the U.S. who have served on these week long mission teams have been blessed to have worked with the Honduran people of the Agalta Valley. I had the privilege and honor to have been a part of several teams led by the late Pastor Ron Campbell from Tarrytown United Methodist Church in Austin, Texas. Jeri Campbell still serves as part of the mission education teams joining with HOI and Tarrytown United Methodist Church. Jeri is an accomplished artist and first started painting scenes depicting the Agalta Valley. Thanks to Jeri for providing the front cover art of *A Golfer's Beatitude.*

Please consider making a donation to HOI to continue this organization's wonderful work in Honduras and now also in Nicaragua. To learn more see www.hoi.org

If you know golf, my prayer is that you would also know Jesus Christ. Feel free to discuss either golf or Christ or both with me at JohnFincherAuthor@gmail.com or in the Reviews-Blog section of my website.

www.johnfincherauthor.com

Blessings,
John Fincher

www.ingramcontent.com/pod-product-compliance
Lightning Source LLC
Chambersburg PA
CBHW051835040426
42447CB00006B/536